Sparkle's Sparkle

OrangeBooks Publication

1st Floor, Rajhans Arcade, Mall Road, Kohka, Bhilai, Chhattisgarh 490020

Website: **www.orangebooks.in**

© Copyright, 2024, Author

All rights reserved. No part of this book may be reproduced, stored in a retrieval system, or transmitted, in any form by any means, electronic, mechanical, magnetic, optical, chemical, manual, photocopying, recording or otherwise, without the prior written consent of its writer.

First Edition, 2024

ISBN: 978-93-6554-847-1

SPARKLE'S SPARKLE

MISHKA GUPTA

OrangeBooks Publication
www.orangebooks.in

This book is dedicated to my mom, dad, my sister Disha Di and Shaurya, my little brother.

-Mishka

Content

Chapter One
　　The Beginning 1

Chapter Two
　　Work 13

Chapter Three
　　Stuck 15

Chapter Four
　　A Strange Guest......................................26

Chapter Five
　　The Salon 38

Chapter Six
　　The Sleepover 45

Chapter Seven
　　Mermaid 53

Chapter Eight

The Bird Fight 63

Chapter Nine

An Explanation 73

Chapter Ten

The Real Sleepover Fun Has Just Begun! 81

Chapter Eleven

Going In The Water 102

Chapter Twelve

More Half-Sea-And-Land Dragons.............117

Chapter Thirteen

The Rude Mermaid..................................127

Chapter Fouteen

Cackle! 135

Chapter One
The Beginning

It was one of the coldest winters of Unicorn Kingdom. Unicorn Kingdom was a beautiful place, away from the humans, which the good creatures-Fairies, Fairas (Male Fairies) good witches and wizards usually called NML's (Non-Magical Lot).

Outside, some good creatures were petting animals, others were exercising, and some were playing, chatting. While others, inside were sitting with a blanket, and a cup of hot chocolate in their hand.

Sparkle, a tall, slim girl with long hair, in the shade of brown, with pink at the bottom was sitting on a bench.

She was waiting for her friends- Allexander, Andre, Viktor, Lavender, and Bella.

"When are they going to arrive? It has literally been ten minutes; it is so exhausting that I have to wait for them every day." Sparkle thought.

Sparkle knew she was special, but she did not want to feel like it, the reason she was special was that, that there was a prophecy about her, that she will be the one to kill Cackle, the queen of Evil Creatures.

The reason Sparkle knew all this was because her aunt clearly refused to tell her lies.

She clearly knew that when she was two, Cackle came to kill her, but for some reason, she could not kill her, her parents died protecting her. Last time Cackle came, she swore to come back.

"Now it has been fifteen minutes."

"Hey!" Yelled a girl with blue-black hair

"Bella! Where were you and Lavender? You are not normally late."

"Yeah, mom said that I have to take out my little brother, Mell for a walk, I mean he is three." Bella said.

"And I just woke up late." Lavender said.

"A letter for Miss Sparkle Octavious." It was the postman, Flashy.

"Hey Flashy, a letter, from who?" Sparkle asked.

"Hasley Shake." Flossy replied.

"Hasley Shake? That is Andre and Viktor's mother!" Sparkle gasped.

"Let us open it." Bella said.

As Sparkle opened it, a message was written with a beautiful handwriting.

Sparkle, I am Andre and Viktor's mother, I do not mean to bother you, but I just wanted to say/ask that, we were gone in a marriage of my sister. We came back at 5 a.m. last night, we are not in town, we had to go for some emergency, at work, so do not worry about the boys. And can you please wake them at ten a.m., they will not wake up before that, or maybe not then, but you MUST wake them up till ten thirty. They are sleepy heads. Contact me with the number 568910, if you have any questions.

THANKS,

HASLEY SHAKE

P.S. I hope I am not bothering you.

"Okay, I was not expecting that, but why would we be worried about them." Bella said

"You are not the only one." Lavender said.

"Why did she said us, I mean, there's got to be some relatives you know." Bella said

"I wonder why didn't she use a phone?" Sparkle wondered aloud.

"Because she doesn't have your number. But she does know that every day, at this time, we come to the garden. Because Viktor and Andre come." Bella said.

"Now. It is eight thirty, and Allexander has not come yet." Bella said.

"Hi guys!" A tall boy with black hair came out.

"Allexander where were you?" Sparkle asked.

"I have gotten a new phone, I played on it this morning I lost the track of time, when I saw the time, I rushed over here, with my skateboard." Allexander replied.

"First, we all come here with a cycle or something. Second, so irresponsible." Sparkle grumbled.

"What's the brand of your new phone?" Bella asked.

"It is a new Fairypeace sixth." Said Allexander.

"Wow that is new, and I still have a Uni-seven." Bella said, astonishingly.

"OKAY, so-"

"A letter and a parcel for Bella Heights." It was Flossy, the postman.

"A letter and a parcel?" Bella asked confused. "No one ever sends me letter, and parcel? I-I did not order anything!"

"Here." Flossy said and handed Bella her letter and parcel, and left.

"Let me open it, I am opening the letter first." Bella said.

As Bella opened it, she said, "this writing, it is my mom's!"

Inside, there was an elegant writing that said –

Bella, my little forgetful girl, you forgot your phone, it is in the parcel for you.

MOM

"Oh, I guess I just forgot my phone, it is in the parcel." Bella said aloud.

"What can we do, I am so bored!" Lavender groaned.

"Who knows?" Sparkle moaned.

"Maybe we can do something-something-like…um reading a novel." Bella said (Who was quite studious.)

"Are you CRAZY?! I mean that, is the exact opposite of fun, BORING! Sparkle shot.

"Then what can we do? And for your kind info, I was just suggesting, and you know I love reading, and things, that YOU people eventually find BORING! Duh!" Bella snapped.

"Hey, just calm down, shouting and yelling will not do anything!" Lavender said calmly.

"Yeah, but she yelled fir- Hey mom what are you doing here?" Bella asked her mom, who appeared out of nowhere.

"Oh, hey sweetie, and did you get your parcel?" Bella's mom asked Bella.

"Yes, I did." Bella smiled.

"Who is he?" Sparkle asked Bella's mom

"That is Mell, Bella's Little brother. Didn't Bella tell you about him, Honey?" Bella's mom (Celestia Heights) said.

"Nope." Sparkle replied.

Bella tried to change the subject.

"So, mom, anyway, can you get me a moving map." Bella asked.

"They are expensive, but yeah, you haven't asked us anything since your birthday last year, you make do with your pocket money so, yeah, sure. Celestia said.

"Goo-goo gah-gah." Said Mell (Bella's brother.)

"Aw, how cute!" Lavender cooed.

Guys! It is almost ten, we should go!" Bella cried

"Of course, bye Ms. Heights." Sparkle said rushing.

"Ms. Heights, I have a question. Allexander said.

"What, my dear?" Celestia said.

"What's a moving map?" Allexander asked.

"It's a map, that is… if there are any changes in the country, so it will make changes itself." Celestia smiled

"Come on, Allexander!" Sparkle called.

"Yeah, coming!" Allexander said.

Allexander rushed to catch the girls ahead.

Finally, they reached Andre and Viktor's house.

When they went inside and walked a few steps, Bella cried "This house is like a maze! Does anyone know the way around here?"

"I do, but only of Viktor's room, not Andre." Allexander said.

"Well then, what are you waiting for?" Lavender huffed.

"I think, right, now straight, and the second left." Allexander said as he tried to guide them. "Oh-oh, I think we are lost." Allexander cried.

"You think, we are. Maybe I can ask Ms. Shake for directions I have her number." Sparkle said.

"Yeah, do all right." Lavender said.

Sparkle took the letter out of her pocket and called Hasley Shake.

"Hello, this is Sparkle, Sparkle Octavious. Yeah, we have not. Because we are lost in your house of mazes. Location? Yeah, sure." Sparkle said on the phone call.

"Guys, we have to send our location, can anyone?" Sparkle whispered to her friends.

"I do!" Bella cried.

"Do it then, Bella." Sparkle said to Bella as she handed Bella her phone.

"Done!" Bella cried, and handed Sparkle her phone.

"Great!" Sparkle smiled.

"Hello, Ms. Shake, I have sent you, our location. Sparkle said "Follow me, guys."

"Right, left, straight ahead, Viktor's room." Sparkle said.

"At last, we reached Viktor's room!" Bella cried while doing an air punch.

"OKAY, let's wake them up, we have a lot to do in our holidays." Sparkle sighed.

Sparkle goes to a school called Peace Valley, in Peace Valley, there are her holidays going on of seven weeks, today is day three.

"Hello, you've guests." Lavender tried to wake Viktor up.

"You're getting a set of books today." Bella said.

Sparkle shot a confusing look at her.

"You're strange." Allexander said.

"You know, I always come at the top of our class in every subject, while your rank is top ten or something. And yeah, Viktor gets lesser rank then me, he is in top three or something." Bella said.

The moment she said that Viktor woke up. "Must get first this year!"

"We got a letter from your mother.," Sparkle showed him the letter.

"Oh, yeah right, Aall, I got to show you somethin." Viktor said to Allexander.

"This;" Viktor picked up a basketball, and opened it "Look, a basketball with storage for mini books in it."

"Where did you get that?" Allexander asked.

"A gift from my aunt, wait till you see Andre's" Viktor said.

"Speaking of which, where is Andre's room?" Bella said.

"Across from mine." Viktor said. "I'll go get dressed, you wake up Andre, and then, after taking a shower, we'll both come to the community garden."

"OKAY" Sparkle said. "Guys, let's go."

"Andre, wake up." Lavender said.

"Andre, you are getting a new phone." Sparkle said.

"What! I am?!" Andre woke up.

"No, you are not, now get up and take a shower! Bella snapped.

"K, fine! But you do not need to be rude, all right." Andre grumbled.

"Take a shower and meet us in the garden. Viktor is doing the same." Allexander said.

The community garden was good, once, but in the war, where Sparkle's parents died, it turned bad. With the animals, good creatures, greenery, colors gone, the community garden looked like an abandoned, filthy, place of evil creatures. Many had tried fixing it, no one could.

Sparkle and her friends were trying to restore it in their holidays.

So, Sparkle what should we do today? Bella asked.

"Believe me, I've the exact idea of what to do, ANIMALS!" Sparkle said joyfully. "Animals are helpless, if we help them, then they would be nice to us, if we harm them, they would harm us."

In Unicorn Kingdom, there are animals like-

DRAGONS- These are sweet and nice animals that can only grow up to be seven feet tall, not more than that. They can fly, and can be used for riding. The baby is of one to three feet. They are purple in color, and their scales are blue. (Any shade of purple and blue.) And they can also be counted as a bird, because they can fly. A baby doesn't have wing, but develops them, as it grows up.

BUNNYCORNS- These are little balls of fur and joy that wander everywhere, and like fluffy and colorful things. When they are walking, they look like little fluff balls are walking. They are very cute. They have a horn, and can perform magic.

UNICORNS- Often found in many colors. They are used in riding. They can be in any light color.

PEGAUSES- They are flying Unicorns, but they don't have a horn, they can be in any light color. They can also be counted as birds.

ALICORNS- A mixture of unicorns and Pegasus, they can fly and perform magic.

HATCHI-CORN-They are cute, little animals; their skin is glittery, and they can be of any color, with pale white at the bottom. They have horns, and can perform magic. They are very small creatures, they are only of seven inches, not more, a baby is of one to three inches. They are often found in the color of pink.

FLUFFY PUFFS- They are cute little creatures found in the shade of white, with fluffy fur.

There are also many birds there-

PHOENIXES- They are mythical birds that have a flaming red skin and a golden beak. It is told that a phoenix's beak is of pure gold.

SNOWY OWLS- A snowy owl is only white in color, sometimes pink from the bottom, it is known that Unicorn Kingdom's owls sleep during the night. Not the day. Unicorn Kingdom's owls do not hunt, they are vegetarian.

PEACE BIRDS- They are the kinds of birds that love peace. They cannot carry heavy loads, but they can fight. Most people do not dare to fight with a peace bird! A Peace Bird is also used as a house pet. Peace Birds are also very mature.

The aqua creatures in Unicorn Kingdom are-

SEA DRAGONS- They are also little dragons, who live in the sea, they are in the shades of sea green and blue. Although, it is known that an adult sea dragon can be enormous, up to fifty to seventy feats! But sea dragons are gentle, they do not harm anyone, unless someone angers them on purpose, or try to harm them, or babies and eggs. They also can see whose mind is clear, and whose is not, what is accident, and what is not.

DOLPHINS- There are only pink and blue dolphins in Unicorn Kingdom.

GEMSTONE DOLPHINS- They are the dolphins with a beautiful marking on their backs, they can be in any shade of pink, blue, orange, bright yellow. (You get it, right? Bright colors.)

GEMSTONE SEA- UNICORNS- They are seahorses, with a horn, they can be in the shade of blue, purple, and pink. Their skin is a bit glittery.

FISHES- They are not regular fishes, they are bright, rainbow fishes, that can light up.

"Hey, we've arrived!" Viktor said.

"Oh, hi, so today, we are going to help the animals." Sparkle said.

"ANDRE, LAVENDER- Can you *please* bring food for the animals, they all seem very hungry."

"Of course!" They both replied.

"VIKTOR, BELLA- Can you stay here and build stables, huts, and all for animals (with magic of course), what-ever home they live in?"

"Sure." They replied.

"I AND ALLEXANDER- We will go and bring some clothes and accessories for the animals. It will be enchanting!"

"Let's go." Sparkle boomed.

Chapter Two
Work

"Hmmm... so I will do the stables, can you do the mini egg-shaped huts with a horn on the top, for the hatchicorns?" Viktor asked Bella.

"Yeah, sure, and in no time, this place is going to be beautiful! Bella said happily.

As they both worked, they begin to chat.

"When are they going to come?" Bella asked.

"I Dunno, who knows?" Viktor said.

"Viktor you are building the stables too enclosed!" Bella said. "Here let me show you."

Bella waved and whooshed her wand, and then she pointed it to the stables. She muttered "Spacio" then the stable moved a bit and thudded.

"See, do a bit wider, even a dolphin wouldn't fit in there."

"This is not the place for dolphins, is it? They live in lakes."

"Well, the lake is all muddy, no dolphin or any sea creature would want to live in there. Unless, we clean the lake and get it joined to the other lakes, rivers, and oceans." Bella said.

Viktor nodded, and smirked, then he said "nah, not now, first, let's finish building things, then we can purify the lake."

"OKAY, fine. Oh! Here Lavender and Andre come." Bella.

In Unicorn Kingdom, the ocean and seas do not have saline water.

Chapter Three
Stuck

"Hey guys, sorry we took so much time we- WHAT! YOU HAVEN'T EVEN FINISHED BUILDING THE STABLES! It has been an HOUR!" Andre shouted.

"We know, we were just you know, um… chatting about the sea creatures, that how much we need to clear this lake, it is so much muddy, and uh dirty." Viktor said "And please, don't shout!" He added scornfully.

"Whatever" Lavender murmured

"Not whatever! Do not be rude to each other, it is not the good creature way! Evil creatures do that! Are you evil or good?" Bella shot, trying to finish this argument

"You know, if you both worked together, and not chatted, you would have done at least the stables, you know what they say, work together and do the work early" Andre said.

"Who said that? It does not even rhyme!" Bella asked

"Me." Andre said cooly.

"Yeah, nothing to brag about." Bella said.

"Finish it off you two, let us get to work, ya know, Bella teach me how to build hatchi-corn- egg-houses-with-horn-on-top, Viktor teach Andre how to build the stables." Lavender said, possibly trying to change the subject.

"Yeah, Lavender is right, we should not waste time in arguing." Bella nodded in agreement.

They all huffed and puffed to build the stables and hatchi-corn houses until they were done.

"Whoo, done! Finally! Lavender said, (Who really doesn't like to study or do magic, and something like that).

"OKAY, I suppose we can build other huts for the bunnycorns, dragons, and fluffy puffs, then we can start clearing the trees, planting them, growing them with magic, and making bird's home on the trees, then the lake.

"NOOOOO! Not more work!" Lavender moaned.

"Stop being so lazy, lazybones!" Bella said

Lavender's mouth fell open "Who says *I* am *lazy*? *You* are so much lazier than me!"

"Excuse me! I am not lazy, all right. *You* are the one who is not keen on doing more work!" Bella shot, furious.

"Actually, I am too, you know, Lavender was very fast when we went to bring the food, so fast I could not keep up, we had to go over the Lake of Enchanted Dreams, that is why we are tired." Andre said.

"Sorry, um… I didn't know." Bella said as she realized.

"I know that calling someone lazy in Unicorn Kingdom is insulting them, cause good creatures are full of strength and hope and joy." Viktor added.

"It's is okay I-

"A letter for Bella Heights and Lavender Hearts." It was Flossy, the postman again.

"Thanks, flossy!" Lavender smiled and took the letter from him.

They opened it-

Help! Guys! We are stuck! We are in the Enchanted Mountain! Inside, in a ditch, near the Mine of Gems! Bella, maybe your just in case bag pack can be used now! Other explanations can do for later.

SPARKLE

"What! They are stuck! We better go then, come on!" Bella said (Who likes adventures).

"Yeah, but we can't go without a plan." Andre said.

"You're right, but if they are stuck in a ditch, it might be a trap, we have to act fast." Lavender reasoned.

"I do have a rope in my bag, you know, just in case!" Bella argued.

"We cannot go without a plan; it might be the work of evil creatures!" Lavender snapped.

"Yeah, but our friends are in their, stuck, in a ditch." Bella shot.

"Cut-it-of, you two!" Viktor said, annoyed from their arguing.

"Viktor is right, arguing isn't gonna help right now, we have to act fast, it might be an evil creature work, I say that we go without a plan, I agree with Bella." Andre said.

"Me too." Viktor said. "I also agree with Bella."

Bella grinned. "Let's go then."

"Fine." Lavender said

Bella and Andre hopped on their skateboards, while Lavender took and tied her skates to her legs, and Viktor hopped on his bike.

"I think that skateboards and skates will not do on a mountain, you *do* know that *we* are going *on a mountain, not travelling a short distance.*" Viktor said.

"So, you're saying that we have to get our bikes?" Bella asked.

"Yeah, kind of." Viktor shrugged.

"But that'll take a long time, we do not have a ton a time." Lavender reasoned.

"Yes, it is true I suppose." Viktor said.

"Yeah, but, we cannot, we… it is true we cannot afford to lose more time, but, unless we are willing to leave your skates, and skateboards here, which we are not." Andre said with a grin.

"Stay here, me and Lavender can go get our bikes, we'll take no time. Promise we'll come back here faster than you can say 'rescue mission,' promise!" Bella said and Lavender's hand and whisked her away on her skates, and she on her skateboard was moving so fast, you wouldn't believe that she was driving the skateboard, "Andre come on, I forgot that you have a skateboard too!"

Meanwhile, Viktor took out his wand, and started building the dragon's home.

Meanwhile, on the other hand, Sparkle and Allexander were still trapped.

"When are they going to come, it's literally been, like ages since we sent them the letter, you think they would have gotten it, wouldn't they? Thank God I keep a spare notepad and pen in my jacket!" Sparkle asked and said to Allexander.

He nodded. "M-m-m-m-monster, Sparkle monster ahead! Duck!" He said in a hoarse voice.

"Duck? where? I thought it was a NML creature?"

"No! I mean not the animal one! Bend, sit!"

They both quietly ducked, as the monster stepped on the ditch, making it dark, then Sparkle whispered "What are ducks, I-mean-monsters doing here?"

"This might be an evil creature work, I think Andre and Viktor's parents work for the Ministry of Peace, I think. Ms. Shake said she must leave for some emergency; this might be the emergency she was talking about." Allexander tried to put the pieces into the puzzle.

"But, the Ministry of Peace have got to know about monsters roaming on the Enchanted Mountain, it is one of the most guarded places in Unicorn Kingdom." Sparkle said reasonably.

While in the community garden, Viktor was still waiting for Bella, Lavender, and Andre. Then, suddenly, he heard a zoom.

"Hey!" Bella yelled from distance.

"We've arrived, Viktor what are you waiting for le'go." Andre said.

Viktor hopped on his bike, and they went to the Enchanted Mountain.

"OKAY, we're about to reach it, according to my *non*-moving map, and of course, my calculations only three kilometers left." Bella said.

There was a bit of silence from them after that.

"We've arrived." Bella announced, staring at the huge mountain covered with precious stones.

"Look, two ropes, must be Sparkle's and Allexander's" Viktor said.

"Now, so, what should we do?" Lavender asked.

"Go up the mountain, what else?" Snapped Viktor.

"Yeah... so, where er, should we get our hiking stuff?" Asked Andre.

Bella grinned. Then she said "You know, my bag pack, it's filled with emergency stuff, and I also happen to have six mountain-climbing-hiking stuff."

"What! Wow, from tomorrow, I will also bring a bag pack." Viktor said.

"Do not try to copy me, just because you want to be in the top three of our next year, it'll start from… mmm…one March."

"How did you calculate that so fast?" Exclaimed Viktor.

"I'm much more intel-"

"Excuse me, but we have an important business to do here." Andre interrupted before they could take the argument much further.

"Yeah, sure let's go." Bella said.

Bella unzipped her bag pack, and handed out a long rope with a hook on the end to everyone. They all threw it to the nearest rock of the mountain, everyone threw the rope into a different height, Lavender's was the highest. After climbing for a while, Andre whimpered "guys, my rope has come to an end."

"Andre! You know you can always un-hook it and throw it again." Viktor said. "You don't even know the, like simplest trick ever!" Viktor snapped at Andre.

"Whatever" Andre murmured.

Andre un-hooked his rope of the cliff with a great effort, threw it again, and he begun to start climbing to catch up with his friends.

Occasionally, someone's rope came to an end.

"Aahh, we have finally reached!" Andre said soothingly.

"Don't come to the 'relaxing part' now Andre." Said Bella, rolling her eyes.

"OKAY, now where is this Mine of Gems?" Lavender asked.

"I *think* that it isn't here, it is on the other side of the mountain, near the *Enchanting Accessories for pets and you*, I guess." Viktor said

"For once, you're right Viktor." Bella teased.

Viktor rolled his eyes.

"So, let's go then, what are we waiting for let's go." Lavender said.

"Let's go we've no time to lose, now Lavender." Bella said.

"That's kind of what I said." Lavender muttered

They walked for fifteen minutes, then, they reached the Mine of Gems.

"Now where is that ditch?"

"Sparkle, Allexander!" Bella yelled.

"Guys! Left side five inches forward." Allexander called from distance.

"Coming!" Lavender said.

Bella saw the hole and walked towards it. She simply unzipped her bag, handed them a rope without a hook.

She yelled "Grab it we'll pull you upwards."

When they came out of the ditch, Sparkle begun to talk.

"Guys, you would never believe it! We saw a monster here, and it pretty much looked evil, not a good monster like Unicorn Kingdom's, I wonder if the Ministry of Peace knows about it, if they don't, we got to tell them, fast!"

"Sparkle calm down, and then speak, now I would say monster? Here? Bad? Nah, that's not possible." Lavender said.

"It is! We saw it, with our own eyes!" Allexander said.

"Now, now, how let's go back to the community garden, then work and talk? And you do have your bikes, right?" Bella asked.

"Of course!" Sparkle and Allexander said.

"After going at the community garden, I am going to write the Ministry of Peace a letter, about the monster!" Sparkle said.

"Let's get back to the garden first." Allexander said.

"And where did you get those ropes?" Bella asked.

"Bought it from the hiking store." Sparkle said.

They all climbed down. "My rope has come to an end!" Allexander said, swinging in the midair.

Then, Andre swung from his rope, which was long, he grabbed Allexander by his arm, and putted him down safely on a huge rock, which happened to be sapphire.

Then, he removed one of his hands from his rope, grabbed Allexander's rope and un-hooked it from the peak, then he stuck the hook on the rock Allexander was standing with magic.

As he did it, everyone stopped, and watched with curious eyes.

"That was amazing!" breathed Sparkle.

"Whoa, I wish I could do that. How you went whoosh, grab, pew, it was amaze!" Bella said, amazed.

"Yeah, I wish I could do that stuff too." Viktor said.

"Thanks Andre!" Allexander smiled.

"Yeah, welcome, it was nothing." Andre gushed.

"Now come on, we got to go." Sparkle said.

"Yeah, let's." Viktor added, who was jealous of his brother.

So, they began climbing downwards.

When they reached, all of them rushed on their bikes, and they headed off, to the community garden.

"When they reached, Sparkle took out a piece of paper, and wrote-

To- the Ministry of Peace

Subject - Monster!

I and my friend, Allexander, were roaming and exploring the Enchanted Mountain, we saw a fully-grown, ugly, and evil creature monster!

Just letting you know. (For precaution).

Sparkle Octavious

Bella read it. "Seriously Sparkle?" She laughed.

"The ministry has got to know about it."

"Yeah, but maybe they don't know?" Sparkle tried to reason.

Chapter Four
A Strange Guest

Ariel

A small, thin and, sweet-looking girl appeared in front of them.

"Hi!" She spoke.

"Hi, but who are you and what are you doing here, I thought no one ever comes here, and we all are trying to fix this place in peace." Andre said grumpily.

"I'm Ariel. I want to join your group, I moved here, from an oce- I mean NML place. I think I am also joining your school. Peace Academy, right?" The girl said.

"Peace Valley." Viktor corrected.

After hearing this, Sparkle and Bella finally stopped arguing.

"We'll… let you know our decision." Sparkle said.

So, they all formed a circle and whispered-

"Guys, I don't know, that girl's got bad vibes." Lavender said.

"Yeah, but the work could be faster with one more person." Allexander said.

"And what is oce? She almost said oce before saying NML. Viktor said.

"That's true." Andre said.

"I know what we should do!" Sparkle said.

"What?" Bella said.

Sparkle grinned. "We should plan a sleepover, and for a whole night, no one can ever hide their identity."

"That's true." Viktor said.

"So, sleepover at my house?" Sparkle said. "I'll call and ask my aunt." She added.

"I think first we should ask Ariel." Andre said.

"Hey, Ariel, you are in our group!" Sparkle said.

"And we are planning a sleepover for you at Sparkle's house would you like to come?" Bella added.

"Yeah, sure!" Ariel smiled.

"I think we should probably seek permission from our parents first." Lavender said.

"Actually, yeah, you're right we do need to take permission." Ariel said.

"Yeah, I've to take permission for the sleepover first, I mean, it *is* at *my* house. Sparkle said.

Then she called.

"Uh... Hello, yeah, Aunt Petals, yeah... I know, I know, what! Okay! I will... I wanted to ask that if I can have a sleepover... yeah, of course. We have a new member. Name? Ariel. I know. Bye." Sparkle talked on her phone.

"Guys, guess what she said yes!" Sparkle said

"Don't get that excited, *we* still need to take permission. Ariel, you first, Lavender, then you, after you, I'll. Bella said.

Ariel called. "Hello, yeah, I'll. I was wondering if I could have a sleepover, at my new *friend*, Sparkle. Long explanation… I'll get to know them better. I'll. Thanks, bye!"

"She said yes!" Ariel said as she hung up.

"Lavender, you call, Sparkle said.

"Hello, mom… yeah, of course not. Can I go at a sleepover… Sparkle. We got a new group member, Ariel. Thanks! Bye!"

"She said yes!"

"My turn." Bella took a deep breath and called her mom.

"Mom, Can I go at a sleepover… it's at Sparkle's. We got a new group member. Why, everyone is going. Sparkle, Ariel, Lavender. The new group member of course. I will, thanks! Bye." Bella said nervously.

"Phew, mom first refused, but then she said yes!"

"Listen, we are also doing a sleepover, at Allexander's, if you find anything suspicious about Ariel, text us, we'll discuss." Viktor whispered in Sparkle's ear.

Sparkle nodded.

"So, uh… girls, get immediately to your houses, pack your back pack, and do not forget to pack your daily wear too, because we can bath early in the morning, at my place. Also, meet me back at my place in two hours, which is seven p.m." Sparkle said.

All left. Sparkle rode her bike to home. When she reached her house, she parked her bike, and went inside. Sparkle had a big house, in her backyard, she had a stable, there were two unicorns inside it, although, the space was of four.

"Aunt Petals! I'm home." She spoke.

A tall, fair woman with a bun and black-purple hair appeared. She was dressed in pink, and blue, a pink t-shirt, with a lower blue in color, and a blue jacket. "Oh, my Sparkle! You're here. Now tell me, what dishes should I prepare for your sleepover? And what time will the girls come?" She spoke.

Sparkle hugged her and said "the girls will come at seven, two hours. And, marshmallows, caramel popcorn, some, cheese-puffs, cheese-balls and more please! For snacks, at midnight. The delicious mini burgers of yours, for when they arrive. In dinner, pasta and pizza, and ice-cream."

Aunt Petals smiled. "Sure!"

"I must feed Glittery! I forgot, speaking of him, he'd be playing with his toys! Or Mythic." Sparkle said to her aunt.

"Of, you go now, tidy your room, I need to prepare the dishes."

(Mythic was Sparkle's pet Phoenix, and Glittery was her pet Hatchi-corn.)

Sparkle hurried to her room, upstairs. Sparkle's room was beautiful, it had pink walls, a beautiful bed with curtains above it, stood beside the door. There was also a wide set of drawers just in front of the bed on the corner. Sparkle's study table laid beside the drawer on the left wall. Beside Sparkle's bed, there was a bookshelf, and a side table on the other side.

On the drawer, a little egg-shaped bed was there, in there, Glittery was playing playfully with his toys.

Glittery was pink in color, he had a rainbow patch from his left side of the forehead to his right cheek, it ended below his ear. Like his name said, he loved glitter, most of his toys were stuffed, others were cute, little dolls.

Glittery knew how to color, paint, draw, and read.

He had his own bookshelf, art stuff, books. He also had another bed, shaped like a human's bed with pink, glittery curtains, and a sofa-chair. Also, a bathtub.

Glittery wasn't greedy, he was very sweet, he was three months old after all.

Beside Glittery, a beautiful phoenix stood. She wasn't in a cage, even if phoenixes fly off, they know how to take care of themselves, and return home.

Sparkle opened one of her drawers, full of Glittery's and Mythic's stuff.

"Aw, I am so sorry, I forgot to feed you lunch at two. I'll give you both a bonus treat with your evening snack." Sparkle said.

Glittery and Mythic looked at each other, then Mythic turned and cawed to Sparkle softly, to make her know it's all right.

"Thanks, Mythic, Glittery what about you, is it all right?" Sparkle said.

Glittery gurgled playfully. That means it's brilliant.

Sparkle smiled. Sparkle fed them.

"Glittery, Mythic I must give you a nice, long bath my friends are coming. Glittery, you want to be glittery, don't you. And Mythic, see your beak, it so dirty. Glittery begun jumping up and down. Mythic flew and sat on Sparkle's shoulder. (They both love baths.)

"OKAY, I'll prepare Glittery's bath first."

Glittery baths with glitter and water, all hatchi-corns do.

"Sparkle took three colorful bottles of different colored glitter, to fill glitter's tub. She went to her awesome bathroom. Then she came back, running.

"Oh, I forgot those gems Glittery baths with."

Gems are common in Unicorn Kingdom, they are very cheap in there. Hatchi-Corns also use pink gems to use as a soap.

Sparkle took the gems out of her drawer. Then went back to the bathroom she grabbed a mug, took a bit of water in it, and putted the water into Glittery's small tub. Next, she putted two and a half bottles of glitter in it.

Next, she went back to her room, took Glittery, and putted him in the tub.

"Who's a good boy, now?" Sparkle said to Glittery

He giggled.

"Now, I must find perfect clothes and shoes for you, and a night suit too." Sparkle said "Oh, and I also must find the same thing for me too. I have to polish Mythic's beak, and make her fur nice, smooth, soft, and fluffy."

She begun to pour some glitter-water on him and scrub him with the pink gems.

"Ah, finally, done. Now I must dry you. She took a small, rainbow-colored towel out of Glittery's small, but fashionable wardrobe. She dried him, putted a bow and tie on him and called Mythic. Mythic came flying.

Sparkle went to her room, putted Glittery back on his bed and went back to her bathroom.

"Now, first I have to fill this bucket with water first, then I have to wash your fur, and polish your beak, then brush your fur, oh and in the starting I also have to brush your teeth with your special brush, right?" Sparkle asked Mythic.

Mythic let out a shrill, but soft noise, for a no.

"No, why not what is left?" Sparkle said. She thought for a while. "Oh yes! I have to blow-dry your fur, after bathing, and then polish your beak. Now I remember. Is it right now?"

Mythic let out a soft squawk.

Sparkle filled the bucket with water.

She took a toothbrush, not an ordinary one, but a one designed for a bird. She putted a tooth paste called *Strawberry-Scented toothpaste for female Phoenixes*.

She brushed her teeth. Mythic was very calm, and she kept her mouth open, and let Sparkle brush her teeth easily. Then Sparkle took some water from the bucket with a mug, took a plastic thing with little holes in it and poured some water on Mythic's face with its help. Then she took some water again in the mug, but without that plastic thing's help, she poured it directly from the mug.

Next, she took a body wash named *Phoenix's Chocolate Scented body wash for females only.* She poured some on her hand and rubbed it on Mythic's fur.

"Now, I know you find a hairdryer too hot, but you have to do it, otherwise you'll never get dry on time. It's been half an hour." Sparkle said

Mythic cawed.

Sparkle took out a hot-pink and blue hairdryer and started drying Mythic's fur.

After ten minutes, she putted the blow dryer down, and took out a golden colored polisher and stared polishing Mythic's beak.

"Done!" Sparkle finally said after five minutes.

Mythic flew to Sparkle's room.

Sparkle rushed downstairs.

"Aunt Petals?"

"Yes, my dear?" Aunt Petals called from the kitchen.

"My room is clean, I washed Glittery and Mythic. What should I do?"

"You can take care of Hans." (Hans was Sparkle's one-year old brother, AKA Aunt Petals and Uncle Shine's son.)

"But I don't want to, he bothers me, a lot." Sparkle whined.

"Please, Shine will be free, he's busy handling him, since he came home."

"He's home?"

"Yes!"

"I'll go and meet him; then can I please get ready? After I get ready, then I can take care of Hans."

"Sure!"

"Thanks!"

Sparkle ran to her brother's room, which was blue, with a shelf on the right wall full of toys, and soft toys. With a crib on the front of the wall.

"Uncle?"

"Oh, Sparkle! You're home!" Said a deep, but soft voice.

"Yeah, how are you?"

"I'm fine."

"But you don't sound fine?"

"Oh, it's nothing, Sparkle. J-just exhausted. Would you mind watching Hans for me?

"I can't I'm sorry. I got friends coming over, for a sleep-over. I got to get ready. I'll watch him after getting ready, I promise."

"OKAY, I know you never break your promise, sure."

Sparkle smiled. "OKAY, bye, I'll get ready soon, promise." She rushed upstairs to her room.

"Now, what PJs should I wear?" Sparkle muttered to herself.

"Aha! This nightshirt is perfect!" She said excitedly, holding a PJs with a black t-shirt, with pink, and thick lines on the side, and black bottoms. "It's mature, I think. And which hairstyle? Uh, a ponytail? Tights? Bun? Open Hair? Braid? I know! I should ask Aunt Petals for help."

Sparkle changed into her PJs and rushed downstairs almost immediately.

"Aunt-Aunt Petals?"

"Yes, my dear?" She called out from the kitchen.

"I was wondering if you could help me with my hairstyle for the sleepover?"

"Yeah, sure I would. But, I'm busy making the treats."

"It's OKAY, we can have treats later, but, my hairstyle's an emergency!"

"OKAY, if you say so. I'm coming, you reach upstairs, in your dressing room, I'm coming."

"Sure!" Sparkle said as she ran upstairs.

She settled on her dressing table's chair as she waited for her aunt to come.

"Sparkle, now what hairstyle?" Her aunt's voice called from behind her.

"I don't know, something nice and extraordinary. Also, fit for a sleepover."

"Open hair, believe me that's nice."

"I was wondering that can we go to a salon? To get my head washed, and, I can do curtain bangs, all my friends will be shocked. We can also buy some caramel popcorns, marshmallows, and cheese puffs."

"But your uncle…"

Suddenly, Aunt Petals phone rings.

"It's your uncle!"

"Hello, yeah Shine? He has? Okay, then can I take Sparkle to the salon, if you'll be able to handle everything? I know, but, you know, I know you're tired. That's why I'm asking. I know you're an adult, and a responsible citizen." Aunt Petals murmured on her phone, eventually, she hung up.

"Sparkle, we can go! Your uncle just told me that Hans fell asleep.

"That's wonderful! Let's go!"

Sparkle and Aunt Petals hurried to the door, hopped on the pink car, and begun to drive.

Chapter Five
The Salon

"Now, only one hour is left, we must do it quickly, and don't choose any other hairstyle, by looking at the cool posters." Aunt Petal said firmly in the car.

"OKAY!" Sparkle said dully

After ten minutes or so, they reached the salon.

"Hello, anyone here?"

"*Bonjour Madame, je m'appelle* Hazel, I'm known for cutting of bangs, coloring hair, and washing hair" Said, a young, handsome Faira with curly, and dark hair, in a French accent.

"Hi, Hazel, I'm Sparkle, also, what's je m'appelle?"

Hazel laughed heartily. "Oh, Madame Sparkle, je m'appelle means my name is in French." Said Hazel.

"Oh! Yeah, and how do you know French? That's an NML language."

"Before I was born, my parents moved away to France, that's why, when I was ten, then my parents thought it was the perfect time to tell me, then we moved back here. Now I'm fifteen."

"Oh, OKAY."

"Now, now, stop this chitchatting. We have important business to do here." Aunt Petals said impatiently.

"Oh, yes."

"If, you're an expert at bangs, why don't you wash Sparkle's hair, and do her curtain bangs."

"Yeah, sure I'll." Replied Hazel.

"OKAY, then, do it." Said Aunt Petals.

"Now, only if you'll follow me." Said Hazel.

"Lead the way!" Said Sparkle.

Hazel walked, and they both followed.

"They reached to a beautiful room, in there were a few chairs, with adjustable seats, according to the height of the person. And, other chairs were there, with a wash basin, behind them for head-washing.

"Sit here." Hazel said and pointed to a blue chair, with a wash basin.

Sparkle said down, and Hazel took out a shampoo called *Star Sighs Shampoo for Fairies.*

"Do you like this shampoo?" Hazel asked.

"No! That shampoo isn't nice! I used it once, and I didn't like it!" Aunt Petals said.

Sparkle shrugged her shoulders.

"OKAY, this one?" Asked Hazel, holding a shampoo called *The Daisy's Swift shampoo for kids."*

"Use this." Aunt Petals said.

Hazel took some in his hand, and then he poured it on Sparkle's hair.

"Aahh!" Sparkle said soothingly "It feels good!"

"So, it does." Said Aunt Petals.

"Of course, here's a new thing I started three days ago, that after every head wash, you're are going to get a discount coupon of thirty-five percent discount."

"Oh, that's wonderful!" Aunt Petals said.

"*If*, you don't want that, here's a new one, cut-n-color."

"What happens in that?" Asked Sparkle.

"You get a free coloring of your hair, with a haircut."

"We'll take the first one." Said Aunt Petals.

"OK!"

"Done!" Hazel said, he finished shampooing Sparkle's hair.

"Now what else?"

"Haircut." Sparkle replied.

"What kind of?"

"Bangs, curtain."

Hazel looked carefully. "There are two kind of them, one is only a thin one, and other covers the whole forehead, leavin' the middle part.

"The first one." Replied Aunt Petals.

"Sure!"

"But I want the other one!" Moaned Sparkle.

"Believe me, the first one looks better on you." Said Hazel.

"Fine."

"How much length should it be?" Asked Hazel.

"It should be at the length of... my face." Said Sparkle.

"K!" Said Hazel.

Hazel begun cutting the bangs, after a while... "Done!"

"Hey, thanks!" Sparkle said.

"How much?" Asked Aunt Petals.

"Four Rainbows."

(In Unicorn Kingdom, there are two types of currencies- Rainbows and Clouds. Rainbows are bigger, clouds are smaller. Fifty Clouds is a Rainbow.)

Aunt Petals handed Hazel the money.

"Thanks, come again please!"

They both went into the car and chatted.

"Sparkle you look beautiful!"

"Thanks, what time is it?"

"Six thirty."

"Only a half an hour! Oh, I got to get Glittery ready, you know how many tantrums he throws, while getting dressed!"

"It's OKAY Sparkle, you know I would help you."

"Really? You would?"

"Yes!"

"Thanks, and didn't we have to pick up things, for snacks. And I was thinking if we can go to the *Brainy Store* to you know buy some books, brainy games, Lego for the sleepover?"

"Sparkle! Fine."

The rest of the journey was silent.

At last, when they reached the *Brainy Store.*

"What do you want now, bring it, I'll just stand here." Aunt Petals said.

"OKAY!" Said Sparkle cheerfully.

Sparkle went to the section where Lego's are there.

"Hmmm, a full *Hogwarts* one, from *The Harry Potter series*, I'll take that." Sparkle said to herself, she took one look at the tag, "fifty Rainbows and eight Clouds, but Bella's a great fan of the *Harry Potter series* maybe I *should* take it, I'm to."

She searched around some more.

"Oh, so cool! A unicorn forest one!"

She kept searching, then eventually she picked up a Hogwarts one, a mermaid sea with their treasure, and unicorn forest.

"Now books!" She went to the books section.

"Hmm… I'll take some novels, and brainy books, that Aunt Petals wants me to read."

She putted some books in her basket.

"My fav's!" She said.

She went to Aunt Petals.

"Aunt Petals, so… this Hogwarts, will you…"

"I'll but, if you want me to, you have to promise that, no things… for two months."

"Fine! And I've taken a few of the books you wanted me to read, along with a few of mine."

"OKAY, but promise me, that you would read them."

"OKAY, promise."

"Reading every day for one hour."

"Fine!"

"Anything else you need?"

"Games."

"Go."

Sparkle went to the games section.

"Wooden eggs painting and decorating for six…"

Sparkle chose the wooden egg painting and decorating, bracelet making, and DIY flower making.

She walked to Aunt Petals.

"This." She said to Aunt Petals as she walked.

"OKAY!"

Aunt Petals went to the line.

"Eighty-two Rainbows and six Clouds." The Fairy behind the counter said.

"Here!" Aunt Petals handed her the money.

"Thanks, come again."

"Welcome!" Aunt Petals said.

"Now, I need to buy food, I think that it is the best I drive you home, cause you've only got half an hour until your friends arrive." Aunt Petals said to Sparkle in the car.

Sparkle nodded. Aunt Petals drove home.

Chapter Six
The Sleepover

Aunt Petals dropped Sparkle home and went back.

"You're home?" Whispered Uncle Shine.

"Yes, why are we whispering?'

"Because Hans is sleeping, and why isn't your aunt home?"

"Because she went to bring stuff for the sleepover, and speaking of it, my friends will be here in exactly twenty -eight minutes and eighteen seconds."

"It's fine, he'll wake up. He's only having a nap.

"OKAY" Sparkle sighed. "I need to go now, because I've to dress Glittery.

"Go, and don't make any noise; while going past your brother's room.

Sparkle walked without making any response.

"Glittery, what will you wear, now? Tell me, and I want NO drama understood?" Sparkle said.

Sparkle picked Glittery up.

"You really do need walking lesson." Sparkle said to Glittery fondly.

Glittery smiled.

Mythic rolled her eyes in disgust, rubbished of that baby talk Sparkle was doing with Glittery. (Glittery seemed to be enjoying it though.)

Sparkle led Glittery to his closet. "What do you want to wear?"

Glittery pointed at a little t-shirt, pastel purple in color, with

Glittery written on the front.

"You always wear it! Shoes an' trousers?"

Glittery pointed to black trousers and black shoes.

"OKAY, I want no DRAMA! All right."

Glittery nodded.

"Now sit down!" Sparkle snapped.

Glittery sat on Sparkle's dressing table, in her dressing, near his wardrobe.

"Hands up."

Glittery put his hands up in the air.

Sparkle took one of his arm, and putted it inside the t-shirt.

She did the same with the other one.

"Head, now, Glittery, please don't get scared when I put your head inside this."

Glittery tried to maintain a brave face, but still looked scared.

Sparkle put his head inside the t-shirt with a great effort, it did take time, mostly because Glittery kept crying every time Sparkle came close to put his head inside the t-shirt.

"OKAY, trousers. Leg number one." Glittery himself put his left leg inside. "Leg no. two." He put his right leg inside."

"Shoes." Sparkle took Glittery's right leg and managed to push his down his shoes. She did the same with the other one.

"Very good Glittery! You did it with no tantrums!" Sparkle cooed.

"And now speaking, they should be here soon, and where is Aunt Petals? Huh, I forgot my stuff downstairs." Sparkle said irritated.

Suddenly, there was a knock in the door.

"Come in!" Sparkle said.

It was Uncle Shine. "Hey sweetie, you forgot this downstairs." He said and left.

"Thanks!" Sparkle called.

She took the Legos and put them beside Glittery's stuff. Books on her bookshelf, and games in her drawer.

"Settled, now I should go downstairs and see if they've started arriving yet. She went downstairs and took Glittery with her, Mythic also followed her.

Aunt Petals had already arrived.

The doorbell rang.

Sparkle answered the door. "Lavender! Ariel! Where is Bella?"

"She had a bit of packing to do, so she said that she'll come after a while." Said Lavender.

"OK, so any snacks?"

"Yeah, I am starved! Said Ariel.

Aunt Petals appeared with four delicious-looking burgers.

"Thanks!" All the girls said at once.

Aunt Petals smiled.

"Petals, can I have one too?" Asked Uncle Shine.

"Sure Honey, I baked extras."

The doorbell once again rang. This time, Aunt Petals answered it. "Bella, how nice to see you! I've heard you are an intelligent witch."

"Thanks!"

"Oh, and your burger is at the table."

Bella came in, she was carrying a bag-pack, a basket, and a duffel bag.

"Why do you need so much stuff?" Asked Lavender.

"Yeah, we only needed a bag, nothing else." Said Ariel.

"These are essentials." Answered Bella calmly.

Bella sat down at the table. "Wow! Is-is that a hatchicorn?"

"It sure is." Replied Sparkle.

"You also have a phoenix! I only have a dragon. And I have bought it here, if it's fine. He's just a baby." Bella showed the basket.

"You can let him out. Our house is pet-friendly."

"I also bought my peace bird." Said Lavender.

She opened the door, and let out a shrill whistle. A pink and blue colored bird came in.

"She can hang out with Mythic, my phoenix. Said Sparkle. "And also, let's eat our burgers fast. Because, we can get in my room, before my little brother Hans wakes up. If he sees us, he'll follow us, to our rooms, and not let us do anything."

It was silent after that; they all ate their burgers as fast as they could.

"Come on, Flames. In basket, promise, only for a while." Bella said to her dragon.

"Love, can you please follow me? Lavender said to her bird.

"Bella, give me your bag pack, I can carry it, you also have your dragon and duffel bag." Sparkle said.

Bella handed her bag to Sparkle.

They all went upstairs.

"We may have one teensy-weensy problem." Sparkle said

"What?" Asked Ariel.

"How can we sleep, with only one bed?"

"I go and call Ms. Octavius." Lavender said.

"OK, go, go, go! And come quickly!" Sparkle yelled.

Lavender went downstairs to call Sparkle's Aunt.

After a few minutes, Lavender and Aunt Petals appeared.

"Okay, now I, this is a simple spell, watch me closely to learn this." Aunt Petals said.

"Fouros!" Aunt Petals boomed.

Suddenly, two bunk-beds appeared.

"Wow thanks mo-Aunt Petals.

Aunt Petals smiled and left.

"Now where will your dragon sleep? And your bird." Sparkle asked Bella and Lavender.

"I bought his food, bed, toys, books and feeding bowls, spoons and all." Bella said.

"I bought a portable bird stand." Lavender said.

Lavender and Bella took the stuff out of their bags.

"Whoa! What's this?" Sparkle asked. Pointing to a small stick.

"This is the portable bird stand. See." Lavender said.

She took the pink stick, and pressed a pastel blue button. It unfolded and turned into a bigger stick; the size of the bird stand Mythic was sitting on. She pressed a second button, and the smaller stick on the top appeared.

"I really need to get one of these." Sparkle said.

Lavender smiled.

"Sparkle can I sleep with you? Top bunk is mine?" Bella asked.

"Sure!" Sparkle replied.

"Hey! Lav! Fine with you to sleep with Ariel?"

"Sure, I can!"

OKAY! Now that everything is settled. I bought a few games for you."

"What kind of?" Bella asked.

"Lego, craft and books." Sparkle replied.

"Let's do Legos." Bella said.

"Which one?" Sparkle asked.

"Which one do you have?"

"Mermaid, Unicorn Forest and Hogwarts."

"Hogwarts."

"OKAY."

"I will also get a Hogwarts one. I also have eighty Rainbows and two Clouds left." Bella said.

"What is your weekly allowance?" Lavender asked

"four Rainbows, after my birthday in September, I got seventy extra."

Sparkle's mouth fell open. "Really, wow!"

"That's a lot!" Lavender and Ariel said in unison.

"I have many Legos and books and maps at home, but not this." Bella said.

"Let's build it is, after all going to be a bit enormous." Lavender said.

"Yes, of course it will be. It's Hogwarts, I mean." Sparkle said.

Ariel looked confused.

Chapter Seven
Mermaid

"You look confused, what's the matter?" Bella asked Ariel.

"What is Hogwarts?"

Everyone gasped in the room, except Ariel.

"You don't know Hogwarts?" Lavender asked, shocked.

"No!" Ariel replied.

"You don't know Harry Potter?" Sparkle asked.

"No!"

"Long, long ago, there was no Unicorn Kingdom, wizards and witches lived in the NML world, there were no fairies or fairas. Voldemort, a very dark wizard was a murderer. Harry Potter went to Hogwarts, his home. Harry Potter stopped Voldemort." Bella explained.

"Now where is Hogwarts?"

"It is… I don't know." Bella said.

"Listen, Guys, I have to tell you something." Ariel said.

"What?" Sparkle asked.

"I… First promise me that you will not freak out or anything."

"Promise!" They said together.

"I, am a mermaid."

"What!" Lavender said.

"Yes, that's how I don't know about them, Harry Potter and Voldemort."

"*If, you really* are, then show us." Bella said slyly.

"Okay, is there a pool in your home?" Ariel asked.

"Yes, there is."

"Can I go in it?"

"I have to ask Aunt Petals first."

"Then go ask."

"Stay here, don't move!" Sparkle yelled.

Sparkle went downstairs, running.

She went to Aunt Petals room.

"Aunt Petals?" She knocked on the door.

"Come in, dear."

Sparkle went inside.

It was a beautiful, circle shaped room. There was a bookshelf, a crystal staircase. There was a twin-sized bed, on the top of the staircase. There was a balcony, with a transparent door, on the right side. The room was blue in color. There were few drawers, there was also a desk, with two chairs, and a cupboard beside the desk.

"So, I was wondering if we could go in the pool, it is seven, and we've two hours until dinner, so?"

"Okay, thirty minutes, only. Otherwise, it's wintertime, you could get a cold." Aunt Petals said.

"Sparkle, heat the pool full." Uncle Shine said.

Aunt Petals was upstairs, on her bed, reading a book, and Uncle Shine was working on his computer, on the desk.

"Okay, thanks, bye!" Sparkle said and left.

"Guys, she said yes. Also has anyone bought a swimsuit?"

"I don't need a swimsuit; I am a mermaid." Ariel pointed out.

"I have three swimsuits, in my bag. And since, Lavender is almost the same height as me, she can take one of mine." Bella said.

"Thanks!" Lavender said.

"Okay, let's get changed then.

Sparkle went to get changed first, and came out wearing a beautiful, rainbow, full-body swimsuit.

Bella went next, and came out wearing a blue swimsuit, like a jumpsuit.

"Here." Bella opened her bag, and gave Lavender a pink and purple one, like Sparkle's.

"Thanks again."

"I'll give the towels, if you don't have. And you can wear your pj's." Sparkle said.

"I have!" Bella said.

"Me too!" Lavender said.

"I don't!" Ariel said.

"I'll give ya'" Sparkle said.

"Thanks."

Sparkle opened her wardrobe and gave Ariel a white towel.

Sparkle lead the girls into a hallway, on that floor only. After a while, they came across a blue colored pool.

"Dive, or simply go in?" Sparkle asked.

"Dive!" They all said.

There was a room, just beside the pool. They went inside it, and it turned out that it wasn't a room, it was a passage to the pool. Most people just open the window of the pool, and go in, but this is the real way.

"Floaties, swim caps, swim goggles or anything, anyone?" Sparkle asked.

"Nope."

Okay, which diving? Low, medium, or high?"

"High!" Ariel shouted.

"Medium." Bella said.

"Medium." Lavender said.

"I'm also high." Sparkle said.'

Sparkle climbed, Ariel climbed, Bella climbed, then lastly, Lavender. They all jumped in.

"Be a mermaid now." Bella said.

Ariel pressed her necklace, which was a pink and purple, glittery seashell, tied to a rope.

Her blond hair, turned into the shades of pink and purple, her legs, now turned into a tail, with purple at the bottom and pink at the top. And, instead of a t-shirt, she now wore a short, purple colored blouse.

"Wow!' Bella said in disbelief.

"I… need help!" Ariel said

"With what?" Lavender asked.

"The whole mer-people pod, it's in great danger."

"From what?" Sparkle asked.

"Cackle!"

"That evil-" Sparkle begun, but Bella interrupted.

"Sparkle! Not the time to get hyper! Ariel, continue."

"So, she wanted us mer-people on her side, but we refused. Somehow, she got hold of the aqua gem, and it's the heart of us, and the good sea creatures. The Mermaid Council, went at all costs to make her return the gem, we battled. My sis, is her prisoner, right now, I don't even know what to do. I am lost. Just, I thought, that… huh, I would find some people to help, I did went to many people, but all said they cannot. My life, too was in great danger, I had to flee." Ariel finished

They all listened quietly.

"That's quite sad." Lavender said.

"We can help." Bella said.

"THAT EVIL, LOATHSOME IDIOT! WHY-DOES-SHE -WANT REVENGE! AND I KNOW YOU ONLY CAME TO ME BEACAUSE I AM THE CHOSEN ONE!" Sparkle shouted, her temper rising.

"Calm, down!" Bella said.

"I-WILL-NOT CALM DOWN!"

"You have to, and what chosen one? Girl, I am *mermaid*, I just came because you seemed nice." Ariel said.

"Okay, okay, I'll calm down, for now. BUT NOT WHEN I SEE THAT CACKLE THE FOOL! THAT-DAY-WILL-COME!' Sparkle said.

"Okay, we'll talk later, now twenty mins are left, we should have some fun in the pool!" Bella said.

"You're right." Ariel and Sparkle said together.

"So, let's have fun!" Lavender said.

"I know a game!" Ariel said.

"What?" Bella asked.

Ariel grinned. "My sisters and I used to play this. That one of us would throw something in the pool that sinks, and the one who finds it first wins, and then they throw the thing."

"Where would we find that sort of thing?" Sparkle asked.

"Maybe, we can take a Cloud, I mean it is metal, and metal sinks." Bella said.

"You're right we can." Ariel said.

"Where would we get it?" Lavender asked.

"We can always call, my phone, it's waterproof, that's why I happen to wear a swimsuit with pockets. Sparkle, tell me your Aunt's number." Bella said.

"265418." Sparkle said.

The phone rang. "Hello, this is Bella... Yeah we're in the pool, I, we are playing a game... yeah. Can you give a Cloud to me. And don't, please don't freak out when you see Ariel as a mermaid, she is one. Sparkle will explain later."

Sparkle glared at her. "Why did you say her? Ariel can transform back! I know you're smarter than the rest of us, but sometimes I feel, that you're also more stupid than the rest of us!" Sparkle said with rage.

"I didn't know! And she hasn't got a swimsuit, you know"

"Good point!" Lavender interrupted.

"Yes, you did. Ugh, but it's fine, I mean we shouldn't lie, should we." Sparkle said.

"And they got to know the truth sometimes, and it's such a simple thing, it isn't a point hiding from them that Ariel is a mermaid." Lavender joined in.

"You're right!" Sparkle said.

Ariel's phone rang. "Yeah mom? We gotta' move? Tomorrow? Six a.m.? Okay bye, I'll come, all right." She said boredly.

What happened?" Bella asked."

Ariel took a deep breath and explained. "My mom says that we have to move from the Fantasy Ocean to any other river or ocean or something cause ya' know Cackle found our location and she is coming for us, so we have to move by tomorrow."

"Why is Cackle after you, when her problem is with me?" Sparkle asked, her temper rising."

"She wants us mermaid's powers." Ariel said.

"Why?" Lavender asked.

"Us mermaid's powers are stronger than all the witches together."

"Girls! Your coin!" It was Aunt Petals. "WHAT! Ariel! Mermaid? Explain! NOW!

"We also didn't know, I'll explain later, let us have fun for now. Please?" Sparkle said

"Okay! Bye." Aunt Petals said and left.

"Okay, guys, I think we should also have some fun, Ariel, I say you save your story for the night." Bella said.

"I agree. What's up for some WATER-PARTY FUNNN!" Sparkle said.

"I'll throw the Cloud first. Rules:

Sparkle's Sparkle

1. No pushing or shoving.
2. No following anyone.
3. The one who sees it first, picks it up first.
4. The person who finds it, throws it. But, they have to consult the thrower first.
5. No fighting about who found it first.
6. The people who fight gets disqualified.
7. Have fun!"

"Interesting!" Bella said.

"Okay, let's play. Close your eyes. I am throwing." Ariel said.

Ariel threw the Cloud on the other side of the pool. "You can open your eyes now."

They opened their eyes and swam. Bella saw the coin. She went to Ariel.

"Bella's found the Cloud!" She announced.

"Tell us when will be the time to open our eyes." Ariel said to Bella.

Bella nodded.

Bella threw the coin in the baby pool, which was full of toys, and Glittery and Flame were there, on floats specially designed for the

Bella whispered to Flames and Glittery. "Guys, I am putting this in, and continue playing, don't tell anyone. Don't move it, okay?"

"Open your eyes now."

Lavender saw it. Then Ariel, Sparkle, Lavender, Sparkle and Bella. They played until it was the time to change.

Sparkle picked Glittery, and Bella picked Flames.

"Pool playtime is over." Bella said.

The girls got changed and they went to Sparkle's room.

Chapter Eight
The Bird Fight

As they got into the room, Sparkle said to Bella. "Our pets really need walking lessons."

"Well, can't argue with that." Bella said.

"What?" Ariel asked.

"We could split into two groups. Bella, Ariel, you are going to walk Flames. Me and Sparkle can walk Glittery."

"Nice idea Lav!" Bella said.

"Thanks!"

"Let's do it!" Sparkle said.

Sparkle held Glittery's hand on the right, as Lavender did on the left. Bella also held Flames right hand Ariel on the left.

They first begun it by holding hands, Glittery looked troubled. And Flames was being grumpy.

That's when Aunt Petals came in. "Come downstairs in an hour for dinner." Aunt Petals aid as she headed downstairs. "And Sparkle, Hans is awake!" She added.

"Okay!"

"Spark, who is Hans?" Bella asked.

"My little brother."

"You've had a little brother and you never told us?" Lavender asked.

"Sorry, on ten February it's his second birthday."

"It's okay." Bella said.

"Let's forget everything for now, and build Legoes!" Bella said.

"Okay!" Sparkle said.

"Hogwarts?" Lavender asked.

"Actually, I want make the mermaid one, before I leave in the morning." Ariel said.

Sparkle looked at Bella.

"Okay, fine!" Bella said "But we've already unpacked the Hogwarts one."

"Here, take this." Sparkle said to Ariel and handed her the mermaid Lego."

"It's really nice of you, but, it's yours. Also, I can't take with me." Ariel said.

"It's small. And you *have* a bag pack."

"Thanks, I'll never forget this. Since you don't have a mermaid phone…" She opened her bag. "You can have this, us mermaids have this, almost every of us mermaid has a human friend, we use this to connect with each other. It can also turn you into a mermaid." She gave each of them a similar shell like hers. She also took out three violet and blue colored ropes, and tied them to the seashell. "When it'll be with you, it'll turn into the color of your personality. If, someone will try to steal, it'll turn in a shade of black did I mention you can also turn into a mermaid. See like this" They all took a necklace. Sparkle's turned pink and pastel blue. Bella's turned blue and violet. Lavender's turned lavender. Ariel's was already purple. She pressed each side of the shell with two fingers and she turned into a mermaid. They also tried it, and they all turned into mermaids. Their blouses, tails and hair were almost the same color as their necklaces. They also had a crown, same as the necklace.

"It's amaze! Thank you!" Bella breathed.

"I promise, wherever you will be, you will always be in our hearts." Lavender said.

"I'll never forget you!" Sparkle said.

"Thanks guys! You can also call me with it, and I can also. If we miss each other too much, there can also be a trail of gemstones and glitter made with this necklace, if you want to find me." Ariel said.

They all removed their tails back with their legs with another press of a necklace.

"It is so cool!" said Bella.

When they taught both pets how to learn to walk, they chatted.

"Hey, we have to choose subjects this year. It's our fifth year! I am choosing History, NML's and Evil creatures." Bella said.

"Three subjects? Well, I am choosing fashion and medical. The simple one, like nurse." Lavender said.

"I haven't decided; I mean so many possibilities. NML, fashion, History, Evil Creatures, computer. So many!" Sparkle said.

"Sparkle, if I know you, you should also choose fashion." Lavender said.

"Nah!" Sparkle replied. "I think, mm… uh… NML! I mean, we… in NML get to study their world we get to study maps, and computer too, we'll get to learn how to use different techs, and all, it'll be amaze!"

"What is fashion, history, and computer?" Ariel asked.

"They are a thing." Sparkle said.

"They are also our subjects at school." Bella said.

"Wow, great things, you, land creatures, and we have subject like, practicing magic, defense against evil creatures, tricks with water magic, etcetera, etcetera."

"Wow, your classes sound really cool!" Lavender said.

"Lavender, our classes are cool too!" Bella snapped.

"They are cool. We have five years, age eight to thirteen, then we have college at sixteen, but my classes are shut down because of, you know, the evil creature eclipse. If we don't get this finished within a month, us mermaids and mermen, who are studying may be a year late for everything." Ariel said.

"That's sad, do you want us, good creature help? We can discuss it over dinner, I am sure Aunt Petals, and Uncle Shine will understand, and you know, good creatures are always ready to help. And, also, Uncle Shine also is known through Unicorn Kingdom, I am pretty sure he'll be able to help." Sparkle said thoughtfully.

"I am not sure guys, if that's what other good sea creatures want." Ariel said.

"Call them?" Bella suggested.

"Good thinking." Ariel took her seashell-shaped phone out of her pocket, and called. "*Holla*, mom, we have some good creatures on our side, they would like to help. Yes, of course! n Ask? Okay. I'll hold... Yeah mom? Yes! Yes!" Ariel smiled and nodded her head. Finally, she hung up. "Guys, yes!"

"Okay, at dinner, we can discuss with Mr. and Ms. Octavious." Bella said.

"Yep, we'll!" Lavender nodded agreement. Sparkle said nothing. Just then, Lavender's peace bird let out a shrill screech. Lavender rushed to her side. "Love! What happened?" Lavender asked her bird. Her bird pointed her wing at Mythic. "Bad bird!" She said to Mythic. "What did you do to Love?" Mythic squawked sadly. "She is saying that she hasn't done anything!" Roared Sparkle. "WHY-ARE-YOU-ACCUSSING MY BIRD?!"

(In Unicorn Kingdom, the owner of the pets, have to bond with their pets, the animal chooses its owner, not the person. If they are bonded, only they can understand their pets, and they can understand them.)

"Well, my bird is saying your bird, Mythic the Monster pecked her." Lavender shot, with her arms folded, and glared at Sparkle.

"Well, maybe Love the Loathsome is lying." Sparkle said in a baby voice.

"Why are you using that stupid baby voice, it's just so-"

"CALM DOWN GUYS!" Bella interfered, tired of their arguing."

"Bella is right, we should sit down and solve the matter. Calmly, okay?" Ariel said.

"Okay, but Mythic did something to my bird."

"She didn't!" Sparkle said.

"Oh well, she did."

"How can both of you say that, you weren't even watching when this happened, you cannot blame both the birds." Ariel said calmly.

"Ariel is right, I'm sorry." Lavender apologized.

"Me too." Sparkle said realizing.

"Now, tell me what's wrong Love?" Lavender asked her bird. She let out a shrill squawk. "Really? Sparkle, she is saying that, Mythic pecked her on the neck."

"Mythic, did you did you do that?" Mythic squeaked. "She's saying that she bit her on the leg, just because she was admiring the bird stand.

"Did you do that Love?" Lavender asked. Love nodded, and squealed sadly. "She's saying… she likes

Mythic's beak, and is jealous because she herself has a blue beak.

"Love, your beak suits you, and Mythic's beak suits her." Sparkle said. Both the birds let out a soft squawk, as a sorry to each other.

Bella smiled. "Now this cake- I mean case is closed, so, Ariel tell us more about your world."

"Yeah, yes of course." She took a deep breath. "As I told you, Cackle now has the aqua gem, we are in trouble. I fled, and now the pod is back together, they are calling me tomorrow, so I must wake up early, and get back to sea, you know."

"That's not exactly what I meant, but helpful, and good that you told us about your problems, we can help you."

"Guys, it's dinnertime. Come on."

Ariel looked worried.

"What happened?" Lavender asked.

"I am worried that if your parents refuse to help me, then what?"

"They won't. They love to help, and you all will also get to meet my little brother, Hans!"

Bella said nothing.

They all went down stairs and sat on a dining table in the living room.

The living room was a nice and calming room. It was also pretty big. On the right side, there was the entrance.

There were a few couches, and sofa-chairs. And a television. On the left side, there is a huge dining table, with six chairs, and two baby chairs, the walls were pastel purple, and there was a collage, filled with photos.

"Wow, this is nice." Ariel said.

"Thanks!" Sparkle said.

The dining table was already filled with a pasta and pizza. There was also Brown, chocolatey drink in a huge bottle.

Lavender gasped at the drink. "Hot Chocolate, my fav!"

"Now girls, I am getting Hans, please start eating, Shine will be here in a few minutes." Aunt Petals said.

"No Ms. Octavious! How can we start eating without you and Mr. Octavious, we'll all eat together." Bella declared.

Aunt Petals smiled. "Aw Bella, you are such a sweet girl."

"Thank you."

"Girls, no ice-cream, it's winter. Okay? And, you have already eaten ice-cream." Aunt Petals said

"Fine, but, only unfair." Sparkle said.'

"Sparkle, I really don't think it's unfair, I mean that if we eat it, we might get sick, you know." Lavender reasoned.

"Aw, it's a pity, I've always wanted to try land dry ice cream, ours is very salty. They say that your ice creams are sweet." Ariel said sadly.

"It's okay, come back in summer, we can have ice crem then." Bella said.

"I don't even know that, if I will even be there in summer, if Cackle gets us." Ariel said, uncomfortably.

"She won't, we are with you." Lavender said, trying to comfort Ariel.

Aunt Petals looked puzzled. "Okay girls, I really need to get Hans, so see you later. And Sparkle, explain. Every. Single. Thing. Okay?" She smiled sheepishly.

"Okay I will, bye. I mean- please get Hans, I am really hungry." Sparkle said, and gave a smile as same as Aunt Petals. Aunt Petals left. That is when Uncle Shine came in.

"Hello Mr. Octavious." Lavender greeted.

"Good Evesning, Mr. Octavious." Bella greeted and looked at Lavender.

"Good day, Mr. Octavious." Ariel said, and joined the staring contest that Bella and Lavender were doing.

Aunt Petals came in, carrying Hans.

"Aww, he is so cute, I wish I also had a little brother, but I only have an older sister, Daisy." Lavender said.

"You can take my little brother, no problem here." Sparkle murmured silently to Lavender. Lavender ignored Sparkle and rushed to Hans's side.

"Chillax, I know it's exhausting to have a little sibling, Mell is three years old." Bella said.

"Me too, I have a little, eight-month-old younger sister, I also have an older sister. I am pretty sure that if Lavender had one too, she'll understand." Ariel said.

"She won't, she loves children." Bella said

"Maybe she won't but still." Ariel said.

They sat down, and Aunt Petals handed them a plate, and put some pasta and pizza, and then she took a cup and handed everyone a bit of hot chocolate, poured some marshmallows and chocolate sprinkles into them.

"Thanks!" Everyone said at once.

"Listen, Aunt Petals, Uncle Shine, we have something to discuss with you." Sparkle said seriously.

"What my dear, you know you can trust us for everything." Uncle Shine said.

"It's not about us, it's about Ariel." Bella said.

"Tell us." Aunt Petals said sweetly.

Ariel took a deep breath. "I am a mermaid, Cackle wants us on her side, we are forced to. We need help. She got hold of the aqua gem, I fled, I need to go back tomorrow in the morning. Help us, please." She paused for a second. "And I also gave the girls necklaces that can turn them into mermaids anytime." Aunt Petals looked surprised, Uncle Shine didn't "We'll help you, very gladly, I met a merman myself, he gave me a blue, and silver thing they wear in hands, I can also turn into a merman.

Chapter Nine
An Explanation

Aunt Petals looked shocked. "I want an explanation, if I don't, Sparkle, you will grounded until your school starts."

"Calm down, Petals, it's okay."

"Okay, I'll give you an explanation. The thing is, we met her in the garden, she didn't tell us then. She told us in the room, that's why. Then she told us the story, the one you just heard. And, you know we can't ignore cries for help, half of her pod, some animals have been mernapped by Cackle, she had to come here for safety." Sparkle reasoned.

"Okay- okay, I think I've heard enough of an explanation, we'll help." She smiled.

"Thanks!" Sparkle and Ariel said.

"Welcome." Aunt Petals said calmly and smiled.

Ariel smiled. The smiling thing was interrupted by a loud noise. It was Hans, he was crying. Aunt Petals gasped. "Oh, why is he crying? He normally never cries, unless he isn't well or anything." She said, in a worried tone, looking worriedly at

Uncle Shine. She touched Hans's forehead. "He hasn't got a fever."

"I-I am pretty sure he is fine." Uncle Shine said as Hans continued to cry louder.

Sparkle went to Aunt Petals side. "I am sure he is fine, I mean he doesn't have temperature, so…" She shrugged her shoulders.

"So, what Sparkle, you know babies don't cry without a reason." Lavender said angrily.

"Lavender, cool down, it's okay. Have some water." Ariel said calmly.

"I am not calming down; it could be serious."

"Lavender, it's okay, calm down, babies can cry, it's K." Aunt Petals said.

"Okay, but has happened?" Lavender said, looking at Hans.

"He poked himself a bit with a fork, it's okay, we all did that when we were little." Uncle Shine said.

"Oh, okay."

"And, speaking of, don't you girls have to choose subjects in your fifth year?" Aunt Petals said, thinking.

"Yeah, yeah, you had to, what did you choose girls?" Uncle Shine said.

"I chose fashion and simple medicine." Lavender said.

"History, politics, NML's and Evil creatures." Bella said, folding her hands.

"NML'S, politics, and computer." Sparkle said.

Aunt Petals frowned. "You should choose more subjects, everyone's choosing more subjects than you."

"Well, no… there are some lazy people in our school, who choose like one or two subjects." Sparkle argued.

"Choose Evil Creatures, it'll come handy to know about them, it'll help you when you face Cackle, and everyone knows that one day that day will come of that final war." Uncle Shine explained, concerned.

It was strange about Uncle Shine and Aunt Petals bringing this topic, about Cackle. *They never bring the topic of Cackle, why are they doing this?* Sparkle thought. "You are right, I should choose Evil Creatures, and I will." She said bravely.

"Now, that's you Sparkle." Uncle Shine said.

"I am proud of you." Aunt Petals said.

"Thanks." Sparkle nodded.

"Okay, now, Ariel, tell us about your mermaid school." Aunt Petals said.

"It's not a mermaid school, all type of good sea creatures go in there, mermen to. Even the aqua creatures, they learn training. Every sea creature has it compulsory to attend the school, otherwise, they cannot be called a good sea creature. It's a policy, you can say, that's very strict." Ariel explained.

"Your school seems interesting, is it nice." Uncle Shine said.

"Yeah, school's amazing, good thing our holidays are going along with you. If we cannot beat Cackle, until the time our holidays are finished, we might get a year late for college, graduation, everything." Ariel explained sadly.

"It-it won't we are with you, Ariel. With you and the rest of all the good sea creatures. I'll get the news around." Uncle Shine reassured.

"Yeah, you'll beat Cackle in no time." Aunt Petals said bravely.

Lavender put her hand on Ariel's shoulder. "I promise, no one in this generation is going to be late for their graduation, from anything."

"Yeah, enough of this now, I was telling you about school right. So listen. We have five years, eight to thirteen, college at sixteen. We have four years in college." Ariel said.

"Wow, you just have nine years of studying, we have twelve years, age six to seventeen. College at eighteen, to twenty. We mostly join school at the age of three, in three years, we learn simple things like who are Evil Creatures, how should we know it's them. How we should behave, and more." Lavender said.

"Yeah, we also start school at four, in four years- we learn identifying, petting sea creatures and more." Ariel explained, cooly.

Lavender raised her right eyebrow.

"Sounds cool." Sparkle said

"You know, when we are born, we receive a treasure chest, with our colors and names, with some things in them, I can show you mine, I trust you." Ariel said.

"Okay." Uncle Shine said.

"Wow, you even get a treasure chest when you are born, lucky." Lavender said, her eyes twinkling.

Ariel smiled.

"Nice." Sparkle said.

"Great, my bag's upstairs the chest's in it, I'll go up and bring it." Ariel said, and she ran upstairs.

"Aunt Petals I gave her, Ariel, my mermaid Lego, is it fine?" Sparkle asked.

"Yes, of course." Aunt Petals said.

"Why did you give her?" Uncle Shine asked.

"After the swimming, she wanted to do the Lego, we'd already opened the Hogwarts one, things would get really messy."

"You did the right thing." Uncle Shine said.

"Thanks."

That's when Ariel came, running. "Here, this is my chest." She showed a small treasure chest, pink and purple, with her name written on it-

Ariel of the Pink and Purple

Gem Shape: Seashell

"I am very lucky to have a heart gem, lucky mermaids get them, no one in my family has ever gotten one." Ariel explained.

"You said the gem was stolen." Sparkle pointed out.

"Oh ho!" Ariel exclaimed. "Us mermaids are born with a treasure chest, only they can open, we have an oyster, pearl, gem, and more things in it, every mermaid has one, including our necklaces, six more along with ours, ya' know, for friends."

"Okay, cool." Bella said dully.

"I wish I was a mermaid. Just imagine!" Lavender said thoughtfully"

"Yeah, but you are a mermaid now, I mean now you can transform." Ariel pointed out.

"Okay, great! I am sorry girls, but go to bed, it's ten! I'll let you stay up till twelve, your choice how you want to spend it, I'll also take a portable table, and put it in your bedroom." Aunt Petals said. "And if you want to sleep later than that, the choice is yours, but you must get up at the regular time you do." She added.

"Okay, we'll sleep late and wake up early." Sparkle declared "Are you with me girls?"

"Yes!" They all shouted. (Bella, Lavender and, Ariel.)

Sparkle smiled.

"Well, that's settled then." Uncle Shine said. Aunt Petals nodded. "I'll set up the table then." Then she took a glance at the chair where Hans was sitting, then she gasped. "W-where is Hans? Anybody? Shine? Do you know where he is."

"Err, no my dear. What's happened?" Uncle Shine asked.

"UGH! YOU SAY WHAT HAPPENED? HANS IS MISSING! AND YOU ARE SAYING WHAT HAPPENED?!" Aunt Petals yelled furiously.

"Oh, err, sorry dear."

"WHAT SORRY?"

"Ms. Octavious! Calm down, please? We can all search for Hans together." Ariel said. Sparkle glared at her, with the 'what have you gotten us into?' look. Ariel shrugged *'What? I am just trying to help!'* She mouthed. Sparkle rolled her eyes.

"Let's search!" Uncle Shine declared.

They all searched for Hans, around the room, but they couldn't find him anywhere.

"Now what? We all searched, but anyone can't find him." Aunt Petals said, about to cry.

"Ms. Octavious, please don't lose hope! We just need to look from a baby's view, where a baby would go, and tell me, did he walk, or crawl?" Lavender asked, making Aunt Petals smile.

"He crawled." Aunt Petals answered.

"Okay, now we need to crawl, if we want to see, from his view, and he couldn't have gone outside, the door is closed." Lavender observed.

They all begun crawling on the floor, and Ariel finally found Hans, under a sofa-chair. "Look who I found!" She announced, holding him in her hands. Aunt Petals took Hans from him and hugged him. "You little, naughty boy, I was so worried!"

Then a little blue monkey, with a golden horn came, his size was about, no more than a foot his body was like a shimmering jewel. Behind him, an orange dog entered, standing on its legs. "Everyone, meet River my monkey, and Shimmer, Petal's dog I know you may not find him in NML's or any Unicorn Kingdom's animals book, they are special creatures, almost every Faira, fairy, good witch and wizard in Unicorn Kingdom has one." Uncle Shine said.

"My parents have that too, but, from where do they come from, I can't find it in any pet shop!" Lavender said.

Aunt Petals let out a hearty laugh. "Oh, Lavender! You all will get one, everyone does, you all will, and believe me, very soon."

"Okay, okay, now, now, Aunt Petals can we go in my room now?" Sparkle asked.

Aunt Petals rolled her eyes. "Okay, fine, I'll prepare the table, Shine watch Hans." She commanded.

"Come on." Sparkle said and led Bella, Lavender, and Ariel to her room."

Chapter Ten
The Real Sleepover Fun Has Just Begun!

The girls went to Sparkle's room. The second they entered, Bella said- "Now let's build the Lego!"

"No, not now Bella." Sparkle said.

"Yeah, not in the mood!" Lavender said.

"Let's talk first?" Ariel suggested.

"Good idea!" Sparkle agreed.

"Ariel, why don't you and your pod just shift on the land until the 'Cackle Eclipse' is done?" Lavender suggested.

Ariel sighed "I wish we could, but we have some newborns, and younger mermen and mermaids, and what about the sea creatures?"

"Why can't younger mermen and mermaids and newborns be on land?" Bella asked.

"Well, cause they can't grow legs until the age of five, everyone knows that."

"We're not mermaids." Bella said.

"We are now, Bella. You know, we can transform." Sparkle pointed out.

"We are but still."

"Okay, okay, okay guys, I think we should not argue." Lavender said.

"Well, yes." Sparkle agreed. "It's a sleepover, we have to have fun, not argue and fight."

"Yes, Sparkle's right, we shouldn't." Bella approved.

"Okay, okay, okay, now what should we do?" Ariel asked. "I am so bored!"

"Okay. Fine, now what should we do? Games?" Sparkle asked.

"Yeah, sure." Bella agreed.

"Sure." Lavender said, Ariel just shrugged her shoulders.

"OK, in games, I have wooden egg painting and decorating, DIY flower making, and… yes, bracelet making." Sparkle said.

"What kind of bracelet making?" Bella asked.

"Meaning?" Sparkle asked, confused.

"Meaning- Beads, gems, or anything else?"

"Oh, gems."

"Okay."

"I have an idea guys!" Lavender said.

"What?" Ariel asked.

"We should make bracelets for each other. Like, from the colors that suits them, or in what color we think of them, you know like that." Lavender suggested.

"Great idea!" Sparkle exclaimed.

"Yeah, we can do that." Bella said dully.

"Why are you so dull, Bella?" Ariel asked.

"What? Who me? I am not dull!"

"Now let's build the bracelets!" Lavender declared.

"Okay." Sparkle agreed.

"But, we have a… prob." Bella said nervously.

"What?" Ariel and Sparkle asked.

"Since there is only one box, and four beds, then how can we…?"

"Yeah, that's a problem, let's do one thing, we each can take a small box (I have in my drawer) and put some gems and beads into it, and then we can sit on our beds, and make them." Sparkle suggested.

"Okay, but, the wire we make from is one too." Lavender pointed out.

"It is true. But, we can cut it with scissors, you know." Sparkle said.

"Okay." Lavender said.

They all sat on their beds, Sparkle sat on the lower bunk, on the right side, with Bell on the top, and Lavender sat on the lower bunk on the left side, with Ariel on the top.

Sparkle opened one of her drawers and handed out a small, purple colored box to everyone, and took one for herself. "OK. Guys, take some beads into your box, measure everyone's hand with the bracelet-making wire thingy, and then make them peacefully, and beautifully.

"You are not a teacher Sparkle." Bella commented, Sparkle glared at her. Bella rolled her eyes, and did as she was told by Sparkle.

First, Sparkle measured her hand, and cut the wire, then Bella's, Lavender's, and Ariel. Then Bella took it, did the same as Sparkle. First her, then Sparkle, Lavender, and Ariel. Then Lavender took it, did the same as Bella and Sparkle, first her hand, then Ariel, Sparkle and Bella. Ariel took it, did the same, first her hand, then Lavender's, Sparkle's, and Bella's.

Then, they begun to fill their boxes with gems and beads, then they created awesome bracelets, for everyone. Sparkle created a dark blue, and a sky blue for Bella, pink and purple for Lavender, and sea green, and pastel blue for Ariel, and a rainbow one for herself. After everyone was done, they begun exchanging bracelets. Lavender had made exactly the same for Sparkle as she did for Lavender, Bella made Sparkle a pink, purple, and blue bracelet, and Ariel made Sparkle exactly one like Sparkle's tail. "You can wear this, even when you are a mermaid. It is the same color."

"Thanks."

"And guys, I was wondering if you'll come with me tomorrow, to the ocean, to receive your boxes, like mine, to the ocean. Then, you can come back here, and you'll also get a mermaid hone, like mine. Then, you can speak to me and the whole pod anytime." Ariel explained.

"Okay, when do we leave in the morning?" Bella asked.

"Everyone will be waking a three, we need to go by five, and the only time left… we need to leave by three forty-five, exactly three forty-five a.m., so then we can reach by four ten." Ariel calculated.

"I'm out, can't stay up all night, or wake that early." Lavender said.

"Lav! Please, I won't be the same without you!" Bella requested.

"Okay, fine! Only because you never say 'please,' so okay; but won't there be g-giant S-sea D-d-dragons?" Lavender asked Ariel. "Well, there won't be, and you know they are harmle-" Ariel begun, but Bella interrupted. "Lavender! Literally, when will you start listening to Ms. Cole, our Care of all Creatures, Good or bad! She just told us last term that Sea Dragons are harmless, they are good creatures after all! Duh! You are so…" Bella said. "Also, I always wanted to see a real Sea Dragon. I even bought my new instant water-proof camera, that my grandma gave me she last visited. Now I can take a picture of it! And then journal about it" She added.

"How are you going to carry it?" Ariel asked.

"I have hands." Bella replied. As Ariel rolled her eyes.

"Ariel, I want to ask, that HOW CAN WE TAKE OUR PETS?!" Lavender asked.

"We can't, unless they can breathe in water." Ariel responded.

"Yeah, Ariel I want to ask you something about my dragon. I researched, but I cannot find the answer." Bella said nervously.

"Ask me anything."

"Yeah, actually, my dragon can breathe in water, he has legs, a strange appearance like a sea dragon and a land dragon mixed together. I rescued him, when he was an egg. But, I couldn't understand that how can he be both? Sea dragons don't have legs. And normal land dragons don't normally have gills.

"I don't know. I have no knowledge about that."

"Bella, why don't you listen that to Ms. Cole?" Lavender teased.

"Because, she hasn't told us anything about mix-breeds. I take notes of her every class."

"Um... you can ask her next term." Sparkle suggested.

"Okay."

"Now, then, we can sleep now, and wake up when it's time to go, or we can just not sleep." Sparkle asked.

"But, how will we get out of the house so early?" Bella asked. "You can ask Ms. Octavious, but... will she permit it?"

"I don't think she will. And, she is trying to get Hans to sleep right now." Sparkle said.

"Then what can we do?" Lavender asked.

"We need to sneak out of the house." Ariel said, and grinned.

Sparkle also grinned and then said- "You are mischievous."

"Thanks."

"But, sneaking out, that would be hard." Sparkle said. "Aunt Petals thinks about almost everything. As far as I know, she I overprotective. So, she has set lasers, and traps. She fears that any evil creature may try to come, and Hans sometimes sleepwalks, there is a gate from the entrance and exit of the stairs, and more, and only Uncle Shine has the remote of the lasers, and the key to the gates and everything."

"Okay. So now what?" Bella asked.

"We jump over the gate, coz the gate is not very big. And we just do gymnastics they taught us in PE (physical education) class last term in May." Sparkle said.'

"Yeah, but what about Ariel?" Lavender asked. "She can't do gymnastics."

"That I don't, but I do know that how to jump over a few lasers, I do that every day. But, in water." Ariel said.

"How?" Lavender asked.

"They are giving us special training because of Cackle."

"Now, what we do?" Bella asked.

"Let's first discuss that should we sleep right now, or should we just not sleep the whole night." Sparkle asked confusingly.

"Well, I sure don't know, if we sleep, we might not get up, and if we don't sleep, we'll be tired all day." Lavender said.

"Well, there is nothing like freshwater to clear your sleep, and that's why, we mermaids are never tired." Ariel said.

"Okay, not sleepin' it is." Bella declared. As Sparkle and Bella looked up at her in shock.

"Since when do *you* decide?" Lavender said.

"Don't worry, piece of cake! I totally used to stay up most of the night in exams, and all, super easy!" Bella said, comforting Lavender.

"But we are not used to it!" Sparkle said.

"Technically, I am." Ariel muttered.

"But-but, it… you can stay up just one night." Bella stammered.

"Fine, I'll. Lav?" Sparkle asked Lavender.

"Fine, just. One. Day." Lavender said in an irritated and angered voice.

"OK. Okay. The question, what should we-" Bella started to ask, but Aunt Petals came in. "Girls, where should I put the table? And, I've already prepared your midnight snacks."

"Okay, Aunt Petals, should we help you?" Sparkle asked.

"No, no dear, it's quite all right." Aunt Petals smiled.

"Okay, please set the table here." Sparkle said and pointed to the corner on the left side of the door, beside the drawers.

"Okay." She said and settled the table, she said. "Apearo!" Suddenly, all the food Sparkle listed appeared on the table.

"How did you do that? It's a top-level spell!" Bella gasped.

"I'm also top-level you know." Aunt Petals said.

"That's why you said you didn't need our help! Sparkle said.

"Yeah, that. And, I also didn't want to make you do any help, it's a sleepover, have fun, you know." Aunt Petals said.

"Okay."

"Bella, do you know all the spells?" Aunt Petals asked.

"Yes."

"What do you want to be when you grow up?"

"An author, or a journalist, or both. I also want to explore and travel a lot, so I can write about those places in my novels."

"Okay. Bella, would you like to interview someone, and start off your job?"

"Okay, sure. But why?"

"I also asked Sparkle, she refused. You have to interview Kenzie Jackins, the author of-"

"Kenzie Jackins! Only the most famous author of The Device of Knowledge: Know All About The Fantasy World Around the World, Evil or Good!"

"Yes, how do you know?"

"I've read all her books! I am her biggest fan, and I get to interview her? Wow!"

"Okay, OK. I'll also come with you." Breathed Sparkle.

"Why now, you don't have any interest?" Aunt Petals asked.

"But, tell me Ms. Octavious, why me?" Bella asked.

Aunt Petals sighed. "Shine is a journalist for the *Unicorn Kingdom News,* we have to interview her, for her latest novel *Know the Secrets of Ghost Kingdom,* Shine is also a big fan, but sad for him, he also works for *The Peace Weekly,* so, he has to attend a meeting, the same day." She said. "Oh, and you can also choose a companion with you." She added.

"I said, I'm going." Sparkle said.

"That's up to Bella." Aunt Petals said sternly.

"If Sparkle wants to go…" She looked at Lavender, who didn't seem interested, and she knew Ariel had to go "…okay then."

"Okay." Aunt Petals said.

"When's the interview?" Sparkle asked.

"In four days." Aunt Petals said.

"What! Four days! I have to make a list of questions, choose an outfit, and all!" Bella panicked.

"It's 'kay Bella, I know you can do it." Sparkle said and patted Bella on her shoulder.

Bella nodded. "Okay. I'll do everything leave it on me, don't worry."

"Okay, I must leave, now. Hans is very cranky, I must get him to sleep, have fun girls." Aunt Petals said and smiled.

"Okay bye." Sparkle said.

"Good Night, girls!" Aunt Petals sang.

"Good Night!" The girls chanted back.

Aunt Petals smiled and left.

"Sparkle! Why didn't you tell her?" Lavender asked.

"Tell her what?" Sparkle asked.

"That we have to go!"

"Cause I know she would've refused!" Sparkle said. Lavender glared at Bella, thinking she would have said something, but she was too happy to notice. She just danced singing "I am going to interview Kenzie Jackins! I am going to interview Kenzie Jackins!" Again and again.

"Bella!" Lavender screamed.

"What?"

"Don't you have to ask your mom first?" Lavender asked.

"Ah, I can just ask her later, you know, she wouldn't refuse."

"Okay, then at least help me with Sparkle then!" Lavender said. Ariel stayed out of this.

"Why? It's your matter I mean."

"Fine!" Lavender yelled. "But, Sparkle lying to our parents isn't cool." She explained politely.

"WELL, THEY AREN'T MY PARENTS, ARE THEY?" Sparkle yelled.

"Sparkle, calm down! Please! They may not be your birth parents; but they treat *you* like you are their daughter."

"So, what can I do?" Sparkle said.

"Calm *down*! Otherwise Ms. Octavious or Mr. Octavious will come!" Lavender said.

"Yes Sparkle, calm down, I am on lavender's side, and you know I am never on her side. But she is right." Bella said.

"Me too." Added Ariel.

"Fine! But you know I could not tell that to Aunt Petals, she'd refuse!"

"Now then, I am with Sparkle." Ariel said.

"Me too." Bella said.

"Fine! Sorry Sparkle!" Lavender said.

"I'm sorry too." Sparkle said. And they both hugged.

"Good, fighting about such a small thing." Bella said.

"Lying, isn't small." Lavender said.

"We didn't lie Lavender, we hid it for a very good reason, and you know the reason: For Ariel." Bella said.

"Not only for Ariel, also because you want to see the Sea Dragons." Sparkle said. Lavender chuckled.

"Okay, okay, let's finish this argument." Ariel said.

"Yes! Now what do we do?" Bella asked.

"Ariel, tell us more about your life, underwater." Sparkle said.

"Hmm... okay. I visit land very much, because the greenery here, you cannot find underwater, but underwater is also amazing, all the reefs, and corals, so great. And the ice-cream there is very salty." Ariel said

"Is it true you can breathe underwater?" Bella asked.

"Yes we can talk too. And now, as I was saying, the ice-cream there is very salty, that's why I wanted to taste land's. I've heard rumors, but I wanted to check it, but I don't have any money."

"The ice-cream is sweet here." Lavender said.

"Okay."

"I love land! I also miss my home and family and all the sea creatures. But I don't know if... will I ever get to see them again." Ariel said sadly.

"That's sad, but life under water may be, exciting?" Bella asked.

"It is, we travel to many mer tribes. And we even sometimes go to NML worlds, meet other mermaids... it's all so nice."

"I have an idea, why don't you just go to a NML place?" Bella said.

"Because Cackle is going after them too."

"Okay."

Suddenly, Ariel's phone rang. "Hello, yes mom. What! That-that isn't possible! Okay!" Ariel hung up her phone, and tears sprang down her eyes.

"Ariel! What happened?" Lavender asked.

"Cackle got our queen, my sister, father, little brother. My mother is only left, and me. Even the Sea Dragons can't stop Cackle now!" Ariel said, crying.

"What! How?" Sparkle said shocked.

Ariel sighed. "Cackle has kidnapped all the dragons. It's terrible!"

"Ariel, we are not going tomorrow, just to receive our boxes." Sparkle said.

"What! Sparkle!" Bella said, shocked.

"We'll also help you." Sparkle said.

"You can't it's a great risk!" Ariel said.

"What's life without a little risk?" Sparkle said.

Suddenly a black owl swooped in, out of Sparkle's balcony, carrying a letter.

"Letter? Who does that, especially with an owl?" Bella said.

"An ink-black owl, Evil Creature!" Sparkle gasped. But the owl dropped the message on Sparkle's table and left. Sparkle opened the letter, inside there was a message-

Sparkle, I know that mermaid is hiding with you, I am coming for you, YOU are POWERLESS, surrender, or face your death, as well as your little friends' hmm. Let's see, if you are to surrender, hand me... hand me your weapon. Don't pretend, I know you have it, the weapon, the mighty Wand of Power, as well as your little, friend Ariel.

Wish you a hateful and terrible day.

Dishonored,

X

Cackle
Queen of Evil Creatures

"What? What Wand of Power? And I am not going to surrender. And what is with this?" Sparkle said and pointed to the X thing before Cackle's signature.

"That." Said Bella. "Is the greatest dishonor you can ever have,

the official sign of the Ministry of Scares and Dark. Cackle leads it. It is used on important letters only."

"Okay."

"Yeah, who cares." Lavender said.

"Guys, we need to keep Ariel safe." Bella said. "Sparkle discuss it with Ms. and Mr. Octavious, that we're going to live in water for a few days."

Sparkle's eyes widened. "But the interview is also in four days, and we all have to discuss with our parents, well aunts and uncles you know."

"What if they refuse?" Lavender asked.

"We come anyway." Sparkle said seriously.

"Okay." Bella nodded.

"I'll text Aunt Petals, she'll come in our, I mean- my room, with Uncle Shine." Sparkle said, and texted: 'Aunt

Petals, we really need to talk, can you come in my room, after Hans sleeps, with Uncle Shine? Or I can also come in your room.'

"Bella, is Kenzie Jackins really your favorite author?" Lavender asked.

"Yes." Bella replied.

"I don't like her, it's all about different places, NMLs, history, animals, trees, and more. I would like her if there were fantasy novels, or something imaginable." Lavender said.

"Well, that's the kind of novels I prefer. Even though I do have a few graphic and fantasy novels at home." Bella said.

"Okay." Lavender said. "My favorite author is Jett McLaren."

"Jett McLaren? Oh, yes! I love his new novel *The Battle*." Sparkle said. "But my fav is… Jo Shell."

"Me too!" Bella said. "Jo Shell is my fourth favorite author. Anyway, Sparkle show us your book collection."

"Sure." Sparkle said and begun pulling out her book. *Lazy is not nice by C.H Horns, Guide through Unicorn Kingdom by Scale Gilson, The Sofi and Awesome Blossom by Blossom Flower,* and many more novels, they all counted the novels, Sparkle had seventeen.

"Seventeen, okay." Bella said.

"Isn't- isn't there a Blossom Flower in our school?" Lavender asked.

"There is." Sparkle said. "But it doesn't mean it's her…"

"It might be." Bella said.

"We can just ask her, she's one of my best friends." Lavender said, crossing her arms.

"I thought we were your best friends. You know, me and Sparkle?" Bella asked.

Lavender sighed. "Aw, come on! You are my BFF'S, she is my best friend."

"Kind of a same thing you know, and, if she is even your best friend, wouldn't she tell you that she has written a novel?" Sparkle demanded.

"First, not the same thing, BFF: Best Friends Forever, Best friend: not forever! Second: She does like to keep a low profile, and that book is, there are barely like, thirty pages, and there are so many pictures and all. So-called book!" She picked up the book and flipped through it. "It's a six-year old's tale." Lavender muttered angrily.

They were all lost for words, and that's when Aunt Petals and Uncle Shine came in.

"What was that you wanted to talk?" Uncle Shine asked.

Sparkle took a deep breath. "The thing is, Ariel and her whole pod is in danger, we have to help."

"Danger from what exactly?" Aunt Petals asked.

"Cackle, we are in danger from her. She got my sister, brother and father, she kidnapped all the Sea Dragons, they are going there, with me, to protect me." Ariel said.

"When?" Uncle Shine asked.

"Tomorrow, night, morning, around three-forty something." Bella answered. "And don't worry, won't miss the interview." She added.

"But you are putting yourself in danger." Aunt Petals and Uncle Shine said.

"It was my destiny, Uncle." Sparkle said.

"We allow you, Sparkle, but we cannot allow Bella and Lavender, only their parents can." Uncle Shine said seriously.

"Ye- yeah, we'll call our parents, but please permit Sparkle!" Lavender demanded.

"Okay, Sparkle, you may go. But, what about the weather? It's cold. And how long will it be?" Aunt Petals asked, concerned.

"Don't worry, she won't feel cold in water, the water is warm, she won't catch cold in water. And... I don't know the answer to the second question." Ariel said honestly.

"As long as it takes to protect the sea creatures, and the whole pod." Sparkle said.

"But we will be back for the interview in time. I'll ask my mother." Bella said.

"Me too." Lavender said.

Okay, but Sparkle, call me when you need to leave." Uncle Shine said. "I'll switch off all the traps. And say goodbye to you."

"Yes, Sparkle, it's your destiny, battling Cackle, you must go. We love you." Aunt Petals said.

Sparkle said goodbye to Aunt Petals and Uncle Shine and hugged them.

Bella, Ariel and Lavender smiled. After hugging, Uncle Shine and Aunt Petals went out of the room.

"Now you guys ask." Sparkle said to Bella and Lavender.

"I'll ask first." Bella said and called her mom. "Hello, mom, yeah. First: I get to interview Kenzie Jackins. Long Story… Second: Ariel's a mermaid, she gave us necklaces that can transform us into mermaids. Her whole pod is in danger, can I go? Long story… thanks. I will, bye." Bella hung up and said. "Yes."

"Now me." Lavender said and called. "Mom, yeah. Ariel's a mermaid, gotta go with her. We can transform, she gave us necklaces, I will. Thanks, bye." Lavender hung up, and gazed up at Sparkle and nodded.

"Great!" Sparkle exclaimed. "But guys, the last thing I want is you in danger because of *me*."

"Sparkle, we are not in danger, fighting Cackle may be your thing, but we are in this, together. We've been best friends since playschool, and done everything together. We are also doing this because of Ariel." Bella explained.

"Okay, fine but-" Sparkle begun.

"No buts please." Lavender said.

"Yes." Said Ariel. "I know what you might be thinking right now, I feel the same, that *you* are putting *yourselves* in danger because of me, but…" Her voice trailed away.

"Mmm… okay." Sparkle said.

"That's more like it."

Chapter Eleven
Going In The Water

Time passed by, and they all had fun, and finally, when it was three-thirty, the girls were busy packing and chatting about the water. Ariel, who just went to the bathroom and came back stared at the girls in shock.

"Why are you packing stuff?" Ariel asked.

"Well, we are living a few days in water, so we are-" Sparkle said to answer, but Ariel interrupted-

"All your things will be wet, your clothes will be wet, I mean you have your tail!"

"Okay, fine, but I am taking Flames, he is half Sea Dragon." Bella said.

"Okay." Ariel said. "It's three thirty-eight, Sparkle call Mr. Octavious." Sparkle did as she was told and called Uncle Shine. "Hello, Uncle Shine, it's time. Yeah." She hung up and said. "Let's go." Bella took Flames, her half-land-dragon-and-half Sea Dragon. They all went downstairs.

Uncle Shine was waiting for them there. "Sparkle, I'll take care of Mythic and Glittery, Lavender, I'll let your parents know about your peace bird, Bella I'll explain. Have a safe trip, girls!" Uncle Shine said and hugged Sparkle.

"Bye!" The girls said to Uncle Shine.

As they went outside, it was still dark. Bella said- "Guys, what are we going to tell Viktor, Andre and Alexander?"

"I'll leave a message in our chat group." Sparkle said and opened her phone and typed. 'Guys, Ariel's a mermaid, we are going with her. Explanations can be done for later when we come back. If we come back. Don't worry.'

They walked to the Enchanted Ocean, which was a long walk. "This is where we leave, transform, girls." Ariel said, and the girls sat on the bank of the lake, and transformed, and jumped in.

"Whoa, we can breathe in water, amazing!" Bella cried, and released Flames from her hands, who happily swam.

"Come on, I'll lead you to my pod." Ariel said happily.

"Yeah, but I have a question." Sparkle said.

"What?" Ariel asked.

"If Cackle even comes, please, run away, don't put yourself in danger. Please?"

"Sparkle, this our battle too. And Cackle hasn't kidnapped *all* Sea Dragons." Ariel said.

"But I thought she had-" Lavender begun, but Ariel interrupted. "Bella's dragon, and mom texted me shortly after when I said that the Sea Dragons are kidnapped, she texted that they were into hiding, they were found and the animal specialists are calming them."

"Okay, so I guess bringing my camera was useful, yes Flames, wasn't it?" Bella asked, and Flamed gurgled happily.

"Look, how happy Flames is!" Lavender pointed.

"We have reached." Ariel announced.

"Whoa!" Sparkle said, pointing to the humongous Sea Dragon standing in front of them.

"Sea-Scales!" Ariel said. "It's me, Ariel, you remember?"

"Well, I do." The dragon said softly. "BUT WHO ARE THEY?" He pointed at Bella, Lavender and Sparkle. "And, WHAT IS THE PASSWORD?" He roared. Ariel whispered something in the dragon's ear. "Hello, Sparkle, Lavender and Bella. Welcome!" The dragon said.

"Hello, Sea-Scales, I am Bella. Mind if I take a picture with you?"

"Of course. You can take a picture with me." The dragon, Sea-Scales said, as Bella stood next to him, taking her instant waterproof camera out of her bag, and taking a picture with him.

"Good!" Bella said.

"Okay, Ariel, should I lead the way, or you can?" Sea-Scales asked.

"I can find by myself, and I literally grew up here, I know this place like the back of my hand! And you have to stay here to guard the doorway, so you can, just, tell me where's mom? Then I can find her." Ariel said as Sea-Scales took out a map out of his bag, and marked 'X' on it.

"The part where I marked an X is where your mother is, K?"

"Okay, thanks!'"

"And, who might be this little fella'?" Sea-Scales said and pointed at Flames.

"That's my Sea-Dragon-and-normal-dragon." Bella said.

"A rare one, last time I saw those, I was fifteen or something, but now I am seventy, I haven't seen those in fifty-five years!" The dragon muttered.

"What do you mean? Were there more dragons like this before?" Bella asked.

"Yes, indeed, in my old pod, not this."

"We've to find them!" Bella cried.

"I know, but those are very rare. We don't know where are the rest. Where did you get this one?"

"I rescued him. When he was an egg, and took care. We found him, nearly on the edge of a clip, about to fall, on a trekking trip."

"Okay." Sea-Scales said.

"Guys, let's get going, or we might be late." Sparkle said. Bella nodded. "Bye Sea-Scales." Bella waved goodbye to him, and he waved back. As they entered the gate.

"Guys, this is… we are currently in the Glitter Lake." Ariel said.

"Yawn… I am so sleepy and tired!" Lavender yawned.

"Lavender! How can you be so sleepy? My eyes are bursting with excitement! It's so all beautiful!" Sparkle snapped.

"Beautiful *is* right!" Lavender mumbled.

"Okay, now, let's go meet my mother, it's been a while." Ariel said.

"Yeah, let's." Bella said rudely, and Ariel tried to guide the way, then they reached the Coral Castle in the Coral City, in the depths of the Glitter Lake.

Sparkle was amazed by the beauty of the sea. "Wow, all this was here?" She asked Ariel.

Ariel nodded. "Yes, all this was! We have to go into the Coral Castle, Mom is there." Ariel said. "And you'll get to meet the pod's council. I wonder if they will let us go inside." She muttered, still nodding her head.

"Why won't they?" Bella asked.

"Usually, they let everybody in, but a while ago, couple of Evil Creatures came, getting disguised. So, nowadays, they don't let anybody in." Ariel explained.

Bella nodded. "So, what do we have to do to get inside?"

"Oh, that's the problem, I don't know."

"So, you're saying that we have to pass an unknown test to go in the castle?" Lavender asked.

"Yes." Ariel said.

"Well, tests are my thing, and I pass every test, so let's go already." Bella said and swam off towards the castle.

"Bella, no! we don't know what kind of test, you're an unknown mermaid! Wait!" Ariel called, and went after Bella as the others followed.

There were two guards at the door, one of them had black hair, and was tall, slim, and fair, he had a stern expression on his face. While, the other one had red-orangish hair, was a bit short, but fair and slim, he had a nervous and worried expression. The first guard, with black hair held a long scroll in his hand.

"Uncle Fin!" Ariel said to the guard with red-orangish hair, "it's me, Ariel!"

"Ariel, how could I've forgotten you, my dear niece? It's a real tragedy that your father got captured!" Fin said sadly.

"Oh, Mr. Shell!" Ariel said to the guard with black hair.

"Hello, Ariel. And who might these be?" The guard, Shell said in a Spanish accent, and pointed at Lavender, Bella and Sparkle.

"They are the one I told the council about, meet Sparkle, Bella and Lavender.

"Pleased to meet you!" Fin said, bowing.

"*Holla*, Girls!" Shell said, bowing.

"Is mom inside?" Ariel asked.

"She indeed is." Fin said.

"Can we go?"

"How are we supposed to trust you?" Shell asked.

"You can! Uncle, you can even ask me a question."

Fin hesitated for a moment, then he asked- "How old am I?"

"Twenty-eight, everyone knows that."

"Okay, I'll go with you, and escort you to where they are." Fin said.

"No, you stay here, I'm going to take them." Shell said strictly.

"Okay." Fin said.

"Follow me, girls!" Shell said. He went inside the castle. Inside there were calming blue and red-pinkish walls, Sparkle gasped in awe. After a few minutes, Shell swung a beautiful looking painting.

"This is the secret headquarters of the Council." He said and swam inside, as they all followed.

"Whoa! Cool!" Bella said looking at the light blue walls, with purple and green glitter on them. "Isn't it Flames?"

"Yes, it's nice, calming." Sparkle said.

"It so is!" Lavender said.

But Ariel didn't seem to notice, she was busy in her own thoughts.

"Now, I'll leave you here." Shell said.

Inside, there were many mermaids and mermen, sitting on a long table.

"Mom!" Ariel cried, and flung her arms on the mermaid at the center of the table. The mermaid had the same hair as Ariel's, a sweet-looking face, and fair skin.

"My dear, are you all right?" She said, she had a sweet voice. "And these must be your friends?" She asked.

"Yes, this is Bella, Lavender and Sparkle."

"Sparkle, Sparkle Octavious? The girl who'll kill Cackle?" A mermaid with red hair asked.

"Yes, that's indeed me." Sparkle swam up."

"Okay, but I-I-why are you here?" The oldest merman with dark skin and hair said.

"To receive our boxes, but that's not important. The main reason we came here is to join he battle against Cackle." Sparkle replied.

"But it's not your fight!" A fair woman with pastel-blue hair said.

"Actually, it is mine, and Cackle knows that I have more power than anybody else in the world, and endless strength, with my friends, and all the Good Creatures, that's why she's trying to take you mer-people off my side." Sparkle said.

"Really?" The merman with dark skin and hair said. "Are you the cause to our problems?"

"Well, you see I-I-" Sparkle stammered.

"No! She's not! It's not her fault that the prophecy had to be about her!" Ariel protested.

"It may as well be not, but, it's because of her that our pod's endangered! The mermaid sitting next to Ariel's mom rose from her chair. She had dark skin, and dark blue hair.

"Miss Cartwright, please! Even if it's her fault, she came to help!"

"Okay, fine." The mermaid, Ms. Cartwright said and sat down on her chair.

"IF THAT IS A PROBLEM TOO, I CAN GO BACK YOU KNOW, I DON'T HAVE A PROBLLEM WITH IT! FIGHT THE BATTLE YOURSELF! US GOOD WITCHES, WIZARDS, FAIRIES AND FAIRAS WERE HELPING, WE WON'T!" Sparkle shouted, her anger rising.

"Don't you dare get rude with us young lady!" Ms. Cartwright said.

"We are the mer council we can banish you anytime we want!" The mermaid said with red hair, and a very fair skin.

"Yeah, so banish me now, will you?" Sparkle said. "I'll do a thing, before you banish me, I'll go myself!"

"Ms. Rose, please!" Ariel said to the red-haired mermaid.

"Yes, sure do!" Ms. Cartwright said.

"As the order, you won't get your box, and your necklace will be taken, from all three of you!" The merman with dark skin and hair said.

"No! But-but we didn't do anything!" Bella said.

"Okay, you might as well stay, but not Sparkle !" The mermaid with pastel blue hair declared.

"But, that decision remains to me, as the head of the Mer Council." Ariel's mom said.

"Let you just as well know, that if you banish Sparkle, all of us good land creatures are going out!" Lavender declared.

"But what if I *don't*?" Ariel's mom said. "Now, you shouted at us today, we also did. We said everything was your fault, I don't blame you, anyone would have gone hyper if we said all of that was their fault." She said.

"So that means I am not banished?"

"You aren't!" Ariel's mom said sweetly. "And that temper might be useful for when you're battling Cackle."

"Thank you!" Sparkle said.

"Always welcome!" Ariel's mom replied. "And let's start the ceremony, of the boxes!" She clapped her hands, and a fair mermaid with blonde silvery-gold hair came in carrying a cushion with three boxes in it. One pink, second purple, and third blue. "Thank you Gem!" Ariel's mom said. "Now for the ceremony to begin!" She announced as the mermen and mermaids harmonized. "First up: Sparkle Octavious!" She said as the mermaid called Gem gave her the pink box. "Open it!" Gem whispered to Sparkle. Sparkle opened it and got a heart-shaped gem in pink color.

"Wow, look like Sparkle has gotten a Heart-Gem! It means she has the power of love!" Ariel's mom announced.

"Wow, cool!" Lavender murmured to Bella.

"Second: Bella Heights!" Ariel's mom said. Bella swam forward and Gem handed her the blue box. "Open it!" Gem whispered to Bella. Bella opened it. She had a star-shaped gem in purplish-dark blue color.

"Looks like Bella has gotten a star gem, that's rare! It means, she can learn anything, and is very intelligent She can achieve anything she want." Ariel's mom announced.

"Third up: Last, but not the least! Lavender Hearts!" Ariel's mom said as Gem handed Lavender the purple box. "Open it!" She whispered to her. She opened it and she got a circle-shaped gem in purple color.

"Looks like Lavender has a circle gem! It means that... um, uh... she-she..." Ariel's mom voice trailed off. "The ceremony is over, Ariel, you can escort them to the house, and show them their rooms. I have work to do."

"Yes mom!" Ariel said brightly as she led them out of the castle.

"Wow, looks like you both have gotten rare gems, but not me!" Lavender said jealously.

"Lavender! It's okay, it doesn't matter!" Sparkle said.

"It does!" Lavender said, irritated.

"But it doesn't matter more than our friendship!" Sparkle said.

"Yeah, it does, it means you are special, but I am not!"

"Oh, come on, chillax!" Bella said, rolling her eyes.

"No! I-I am leaving!" Lavender declared.

"You can't leave! It-it is not worth it!" Sparkle said.

"It is, I don't care! You are special, I am not, all you three are!"

"Oh, come on! Many mermen and mermaids get circle gems!" Ariel said.

"You haven't! you got a heart gem yourself!" Lavender said highly annoyed.

"You got to stay! I don't care, but you are my friend, and you have to!" Ariel declared.

Lavender sighed. "Fine, I just got a bit jealous for a moment, I guess, that you all got special gems, and I didn't. Sparkle, you were right, it doesn't matter!" Lavender admitted as Sparkle and Bella smiled.

"That's more like it!" Bella said, still smiling.

Lavender sighed happily. "We have reached at my house; I'll show you your rooms." Ariel said.

"You mean we have different rooms?" Sparkle asked, staring at the small mansion in front of them.

"No, uh… Lavender would be sleeping with me, and Sparkle, Bella, you are together." Ariel said, she paused for a moment, and then said- "If it's all right to you?"

"Okay. It's all fine to me, I don't have any prob, ask the others." Bella said as Sparkle and Lavender nodded.

"Okay, then let's go inside." Ariel declared.

"Yeah, thanks, very tired, I am." Lavender yawned.

"One question, how will we sleep, if we keep floating in the water?" Bella asked

"You can, you'll see." Ariel said.

"Will there be a bed for Flames?" Bella asked.

"Yes, right after staying in the water was decided, I called mom, and texted her so she'd customized your rooms."

"Okay, that is generous." Sparkle said.

"Okay, should we enter now?" Lavender asked.

"Yeah, sure." Ariel said, and opened the gate. "Welcome everyone!" She said with a smile.

"I have to ask something." Sparkle said.

"What?" Ariel asked.

"Weren't you moving to another world?" Sparkle asked.

Ariel sighed. "We decided, that we shouldn't move, that would... and we should be brave, and face our destiny."

"That's... brave." Bella said.

"I know." Ariel said. "Sparkle, Bella, this is your room, mine and Lavender's is beside this." Ariel said and left with Lavender.

Sparkle and Bella, both stared at the massive and the beautiful bedroom ahead. It had two beds, right in front if each other, both had side tables. Sparkle's bed had curtains in pink color, while Bella had a starry curtain right above her bed, and a huge bookshelf full of books.

"This is so awesome!" Bella squealed.

"It sure is!" Sparkle said.

"So many books, I mean!"

"Yep!"

"There is even a bed for Flames!" Bella said and pointed to the cute-looking dark blue bed beside her bed.

"Should we sleep?" Sparkle asked.

"I am too un-sleepy and excited to fall asleep!" Bella said.

"Whatever, I am sleeping, don't disturb." Sparkle said and begun to lay on her bed, just as she begun to sleep, Ariel entered.

"Uh-Huh! You aren't sleeping right now, Spark!" Ariel said.

"Why?" Sparkle asked.

"Cackle's going to arrive any minute, you know." Ariel said.

"So what?"

"We must be prepared, come on." Ariel said and left the room.

"Flames! My cute, little dragon, stay safe, I am going to be back soon!" Bella said to her dragon and hurried off after

Sparkle, Ariel and Lavender.

"So where are we going exactly?" Bella asked Ariel.

"You'll see!" Ariel grinned, as they exited the mansion. Ariel led them to a wall a few minutes later.

Chapter Twelve
More Half-Sea-And-Land Dragons

"What's this, a blank wall?" Bella asked rudely.

"You'll see!" Ariel said and tapped the wall three times with her tail. Suddenly, the wall opened and a red, coral pathway emerged.

"Is it just me, or do you love red?" Lavender asked.

"We make almost everything out of coral." Ariel answered as Lavender nodded, and they walked down the pathway.

"We are currently in Rainbow River." Ariel said.

"Is it true it is called that because there are rainbow bridges and rainbows in it?" Bella asked.

"Yes, it's beautiful." Ariel answered.

"Aw, I should have bought Flames with me, I thought we were going to prepare for war, or something." Bella said sadly. "What if something happened to him, what if someone comes in and tries to hurt him?" She asked.

"No one will. Security at our homes have increased, since mom is at the Council, they regularly check rooms, unless you have put the don't disturb sign on the gate." Ariel said.

"Whoo! Thank God!" Bella sighed, the girls swam and chatted until Ariel announced, "we've arrived!"

"Whoa! Beautiful!" Sparkle said, awestruck. Staring at the beautiful rainbow bridge ahead.

"What! Gemstone Dolphins!" Bella exclaimed.

"It's downright beautiful!" Lavender exclaimed at pod of Gemstone Dolphins.

Suddenly, a light-pink dolphin came swimming at Ariel. "Guys, meet my dolphin, Finny." Ariel said and patted the dolphin.

"Let me take a picture of you! Please! Bella pleaded.

"Okay! Fine!" Ariel said and posed with Finny for a picture as Bella took a photo.

"All done!" Bella said.

"Just out of curiosity, why did you keep her here?" Lavender asked.

"There is a passage, in all the water bodies to here, so I wanted to keep her safe, and wherever we go in, I could always find her, and the gate isn't visible to non-sea creatures, so I just wanted to keep her safe, that's all." Ariel explained.

"Oh, smart!" Lavender exclaimed.

"So, why exactly are we here? And what was so important, just to meet your dolphin?" Sparkle grumbled.

"Nope! We came here for many things, but most importantly, I found out about Bella's dragon, some dragons, like yours just came in last week, see for yourself."

"How-how will be get Flames?" Lavender and Bella asked together.

"You don't need to, meet Transferee, a special simple dolphin, who can... what was that word? Uh... can, you know, like transport here and there, like appear and disappear." Ariel mumbled.

"You mean, like teleportation?" Sparkle asked.

"Yes, that's the word I was looking for!" Ariel said as a blue dolphin appeared.

"Okay. Transferee, please get Flames, from my house. Bella and Sparkle's room, okay?" Ariel said and smiled at the Transferee. The dolphin nodded

"Okay, go!" Ariel said as the dolphin disappeared. A few minutes later, Transferee appeared with Flames.

"Who's a good girl?" Lavender said to Transferee. Transferee jumped playfully to the surface and came back down, as Bella hugged Flames.

"Are you all right? Are you hurt or dizzy?" Bella asked Flames and gave him a treat from her bag. He nibbled it happily. Then, she turned to Transferee and Finny. "Would you like a treat? I have very special dolphin treats!" Bella said as she happily accepted. Bella gave them a treat, and clicked a photo.

"Why does she love photography that she has to click a photo every ten minutes, or so?" Ariel murmured quietly to Lavender and Sparkle.

"Well, I dunno. She didn't even show her face in photos a few months ago." Lavender said.

"Yeah, only in our yearbooks, and school stuff, only because it was necessary, nothing else." Sparkle agreed.

"Oh, well." Ariel said.

"Hey, Ariel! Let's go!" Bella came and said to Ariel.

"Yeah sure." Ariel said, and lead them to pink, dark cave filled with colorful gems.

"Oooh! Sparkly light up gems! Beautiful!" Lavender exclaimed.

Bella gasped. "These are the rare gems, called Sparkbows, they are really rare, only found underwater in Rainbow Caverns. I would love to study some!" Bella said, and plucked one of the gems.

"Can you take some for me?" Lavender asked sweetly.

"Sure! Sparkle?" Bella said as she took one for Lavender.

"Nope." Sparkle said.

"OK."

"Okay, now where were they?" Ariel said to herself. "They were last spotted here."

"Wait, I know a call that attracts dragons, it works on Flames, it might as well work on them, I read it in a book." Bella said.

"Okay." Ariel said and Bella let out a soft call, like a loud cat purring, suddenly a dragon, like Flames, but bigger appeared.

"Who are you? Leave us alone, don't harm us, or try to kidnap us!" He warned in a kind, soft, but dangerous voice.

"Don't worry Mr. Bubbles, it's me, and they are my friends." Ariel swam forward and said.

"Oh Ariel!" Another female Sea and land dragon swam forward.

"Ms. Bubbles, I-" Ariel said, but Bella interrupted.

"Um… Mr. and Ms. Bubbles, you see, I also have a half-sea-and-half-land-dragon like you meet Flames."

"Where did you get him? He is just a baby!" Ms. Bubbles asked.

"I rescued him." Bella answered.

"Okay, Aqua! Come on!" Mr. Bubbles said and a dragon, a bit older than Flames stepped forward.

"Meet our little son, Aqua." Ms. Bubbles said. Suddenly, Flames stepped forward. Ms. Bubbles picked Flames, as Mr. Bubbles picked Aqua.

"Come on, we'll let you meet our entire *group*." Mr. Bubbles said and let them deeper into the cave. As they swam forward, a female dragon came forward.

"Ah, Bubbles, who might these be?" She said in a dangerously sweet voice.

"These, mermaids?" Ms. Bubbles asked.

"Yes. And this dragon in your hand."

"These are our friends, you know Ariel? She came before. These are Lavender, Sparkle, and Bella." Ms. Bubbles answered.

"And this little dragon?"

"This is Bella's dragon. She rescued him when he was an egg." Mr. Bubbles answered. As they chatted, Ariel turned towards Sparkle, Lavender and Bella, who were behind her.

"Don't worry, her name is Ms. Whirlpool, as dangerous as she is appearing right now, is just an act. She is mostly on guarding duty, but when you get to know her, she is very kind, funny and sweet. I know her." Ariel assured.

"Okay, but why the dangerous-sweet voice?" Sparkle asked.

"Don't worry."

"Come on, girls!" Ms. Bubbles called.

"Welcome! Sorry for the un-welcoming at first!" Ms. Whirlpool said in a sweet, un-dangerous voice.

"Told ya!" Ariel said and grinned.

They entered a cool, pink and blue cave, full of light, Spark Bows, and dragons.

Everyone, meet Ariel's friend, Sparkle, Bella and Lavender. And, Bella's pet, one of us, Flames, she rescued him as an egg." Ms. Whirlpool introduced.

"Hello, nice to meet you!" A small, male dragonet came forward and shook hand of Bella, Sparkle, and Lavender one by one. "My name is Cool-Water. Your?" The dragonet asked as Bella, Sparkle and Lavender introduced themselves.

"The dragon introduced themselves one by one, when they were done, the oldest dragon, Water Peak silenced them.

"Good day, Ms. Sparkle, Bella and Lavender. I am Water-Peak, the oldest dragon in our clan."

"Greetings, Mr. Water Peak, nice to meet you." Sparkle said sensibly, while Bella and Lavender bowed.

"What do you need our help for?" Water-Peak asked.

"Well, we don't need your help. We want to learn more about you, and your cultures." Bella said.

"Why exactly?"

"So, Flames here can be happy." Bella answered.

"I think, it's best if you don't, leave him here!"

"I can't he's my pet, forever!"

"Listen, you are young, you don't know any tradition, or proper family. Either, you could stay a mermaid forever, or give him to us."

"I-I can't do either of that! It's- it's-" Bella tried to say, but ended up crying.

"IT'S IMPOSSIBLE!" Lavender screamed. Several dragons came forward, with weapons, but Water Peak asked them to lower the weapons.

"We are only doing this for his happiness, if that's what you wish." Water Peak said politely. Before Bella could respond, Lavender screamed.

"BUT HER SADNESS!"

"Lavender, CALM DOWN!" Sparkle said and took Lavender to a

side. "Lavender, please calm down! If you keep screaming, the chances are ruined."

"WHAT CHANCES?!" Lavender screamed.

"The chances that Bella..." Sparkle sucked air through her teeth and exhaled. "You know what? Just forget it!"

"WHAT-CHANCES?"

"Chances that Bella could keep Flames, or even if she couldn't the chances that she would be allowed to visit atleast twice in a week!"

"Okay, sorry."

"Don't apologize to me, apologize to Water Peak! Who knows how older he might be than us?"

"Okay, fine!" Lavender said and swam forward to Water Peak. "Mr. Peak! I am sorry, lost control! I mean

Bella is my BFF! I couldn't bear to see her crying, or moving so far away from us." Lavender apologized.

"It's okay. I understand."

"So, now. What's the final decision?" Bella asked rudely.

"It's your choice. You have three options."

"Guys! What do I do? I want to keep Flames, but I don't want to tear him away, in this ocean, and me on land. I don't want to live in water, because next year at school will be the best!"

"I know, it can be hard. But you have to give Flames to them, you can visit us, every day in a week if you want to." Ariel suggested.

"Yes, I too think it's right. You have to keep Flames here, they can teach him their ways, and you will never be able to give him the things he needs, growing up. They know the traditions and the right ways of the dragons, they are half of all the dragons, and they are really rare, you know. I am sorry Bella!" Lavender said.

"But she can't give up on her pet like this!" Sparkle whisper-shouted.

"She has to!" Lavender argued.

"No, she doesn't!"

"Guys, calm down! Both of you are right. It needs voting. Ariel?" Bella said.

"I think, you should leave Flames here."

"Okay, if it's voted then." Bella said. She took a deep breath, picked Flames, and swam towards the dragons. "Ms. and Mr. Bubbles, I am giving him to you, please take good care of him!"

"Yes, I will! I will treat him like my own!" Ms. Bubbles said.

"Thank you!"

"We promise we will never make him feel... adopted." Mr. Bubbles.

"Good choice, young lady!" Water Peak said.

Bella nodded.

"Oh no!" Ariel gasped. "It's almost time! Cackle! All of you, please take care! Cackle might come any minute. Please stay safe and hidden."

"We will Ariel. No one Evil Creature knows how to enter, and we have our guards, they will take care of every sea creature here." Water Peak said.

"Okay, we shall leave! Bye!" Ariel said. They all said 'bye' to the dragons and Flames.

Then they headed towards the passage from where they came.

"I am gonna miss Flames!" Bella sighed.

"It's okay." Sparkle said.

Chapter Thirteen
The Rude Mermaid

"Now what we do?" Lavender asked.

"Why are we going back?" Bella asked. "You said we had many things to do here."

Ariel stopped. "In case you didn't notice before, there was another passage just right here, we are going training for the battle." Ariel said and continued swimming and everyone followed. She stopped at a white gate. She opened it, and they all entered.

It was full of mermen and mermaids.

"Here, we train and learn battle moves, since we are going to war, and Cackle is going to come anytime soon."

Sparkle was amazed. There are so many mermen and mermaids, amazing! She thought.

Suddenly, two mermaid in red and blue appeared.

"Guys, meet my BFFs Coral, she pointed to the red mermaid, and Aquariah." Ariel said.

"OMG! It is so nice to meet you!" Coral said in a soft, but high-

pitched voice, then she hugged everyone one-by-one.

"Hi I am Lavender, this is Bella, and Sparkle."

"Nice to meet you Lavender, Bella, and Sparkle." Coral said and shook their hands.

But Aquariah just spoke in a strange language to Ariel. "Yhw did ouy gnirb meth ereh?"

"Sorry, but they are my friends! You should try being nice to them atleast!"

"She speaks opposite when she doesn't want anyone to know except me and Ariel." Coral told them quietly.

"Can you translate what she's saying?" Bella asked.

"Yes, 'why did you bring them here?'" Coral said.

Then, Aquariah turned to Sparkle. "You really are Sparkle Octavious, or a clone?" She said while raising an eyebrow.

"I really am Sparkle Octavious, why would I be a clone?" She said rudely.

Aquariah rolled her eyes. "Whatever!" Then she turned to Ariel. "Won yeth era gnieb edur!"

"We are not being rude!" Bella said, who quickly translated what she was saying.

"Octavious is!" Aquariah said.

"Well excuse me! You first said that I was a clone!" Sparkle argued.

"Yes, so I did, what's your problem? And I was just asking."

Lavender rolled her eyes. "Oh, come on!"

"Yeah, you are probably one of those rude kids at school, who think they are perfect!" Sparkle said.

"Actually, yes I *am* perfect!" She shouted. "My mom is Shimmer Blue Cartwright! The vice president of the Mermaid Council." She threatened.

"That, Ms. Cartwright! Maybe rudeness runs in your family!" Sparkle taunted.

"Yes, it does!"

"GUYS! STOP IT!" Ariel screamed.

"Why?" Bella asked.

"Because, you are both my friends!" Ariel said.

"No, we are your BFFs!" Aquariah argued.

"You know what? You are not my BFF! Or a friend!" Ariel said.

"Mine too!" Coral said.

"I am just gonna call mom! You wait a second! And Sparkle, you don't even have a mom to complain to! Ha!"

Sparkle gasped. "Well, atleast I am happy with myself, unlike you, and I have the power of friends, unlike you, you only have your mommy, ha! You can't even stand up for yourself, I mean!"

Aquariah was speechless. Then, she called her mom using her mermaid phone, and rambled on and on. "Sparkle, I think you might have messed with the wrong person." Lavender said.

"It's okay! We are witnesses here, majority wins!" Ariel said.

"Yep!" Coral agreed.

"Yeah, even if you-" Bella begun, but Aquariah came, and handed Sparkle the phone.

"Put it on speaker, mom wants to talk to you!" She said.

Ms. Cartwright cleared her throat. "Sparkle Octavious, mind your behavior, if you don't you can soon be banished, first, screaming at council. Second, taunting and screaming at my daughter. This is your last warning, if anyone complains about your behavior once again, you can be banished, beware that."

"But Ms. Cartwright, I... she was talking to us rudely, and she asked me if I was a clone, your daughter did. She said that I-"

"I don't care what she said, I gave you my warning. I have important things to do. Bye!" She said and hung up the phone.

"Wow!" Bella said mockingly. "That was *nice* of you Aquariah!"

"I know."

Sparkle just rolled her eyes, and sat on a bench nearby. Soon, Ariel joined her.

"What happened?"

"Nothing. Aquariah! You didn't have to ruin your friendship because of me."

"It's okay, she was very rude anyway!" Ariel said, and Sparkle nodded.

"Okay."

"Let's go train." Ariel said. "Bella, Lavender, and Coral! Come on!" She called. And they came.

The swam up to an area where there were lasers coming from different directions at the sea creature around it.

"First up, we have the dodge the lasers section. We have it because Cackle might throw spells at you, that you don't know and can do anything, so we have to act fast and move out of the way, otherwise, we may get a current." Ariel explained.

"Okay, I am an expert, let me show you." Coral said and went to an empty place where there were lasers. She zoomed on and on till fifteen minutes, and came back with a bracelet. "Didn't we tell you we get something after we win?" She said.

"No, Lavender said and went, she won, and came back with a butterfly necklace.

Next, it was Bella, she lost. "The only thing I am not good at: PE and Gymnastics." She said.

When Sparkle went, she came back with a Bracelet.

"Next, we have the spelling zone." Ariel said.

"In that, we practice our powers. We never told you, but we also have powers." Coral said. "Yes, we have powers, different mermaid, different powers, some of you might have invisibility, some of you might have the strength to control plants, it's different. I have the power to boil the water. Ariel can freeze water." So, it's different." Coral explained.

"So, it helps you find and use your powers, you can each take one, there are seven of them." Ariel said.

"Yeah, let's do it!" Bella said.

They all took a seat, and stared at the screen ahead, who was making them do weird poses with their hands. Soon, Bella found her power.

"Wow! I can move water in different shapes!" She exclaimed.

Then Bella got up as they all congratulated her. Sparkle stared into the screen harder, and tried harder. But, she couldn't, soon enough Lavender found her magic.

"Plant magic, I can move underwater plants!" She said and got up.

Then Sparkle concentrated harder than ever, and finally got her power. "Whoa! I can be invisible!!"

"Let's go! It's almost time!" Ariel said. They went back to the passageway and through the doorway.

"When will Cackle show up?" Coral asked.

"What if she doesn't?" Lavender questioned.

"I think she will. And what's Wand of Power?" Bella asked.

"I don't know, guys, honestly. The Wand of Power, seems familiar, I don't know why." Sparkle said.

"Yeah, it's actually strange. Cackle knows you have it, but *you* don't know you have it!" Bella muttered.

"I dunno, it seems creepy to me." Lavender said.

"Lavender, everything isn't creepy!" Bella said.

"Okay, Wand of Power, Wand of Power! What is that?" Sparkle said frustrated.

"Wand of Power?" Coral pipped up. "I read about it in a book, the Wand of Power is an extremely powerful wand that can also even make you fly, and make you breathe in water, without being a mermaid. Also, it is lost for almost eight years." Coral said.

"Eight years? That is the time Cackle came to kill me!" Sparkle said.

"Um… I don't know!" Coral said.

Bella gasped. "Maybe you…"

"What?" Sparkle asked.

"You hold it, the Wand of Power."

"How?"

"When Cackle came, she came for it, you told us that you were going on a holiday somewhere when Cackle came, you were two. Maybe your, one of your parents had it, and kept it in your possession."

"I don't understand. And the only way to ask them, is taking Cackle's wand. The only way to talk to the dead is to take the wand of the person who killed them." Lavender said.

"We need to have Cackle's wand!" Sparkle said.

"But it's very risky, we can't." Bella said.

"Cackle is going to come here sooner or later."

"No, we can't do that!" Ariel said. "We can't steal it!"

"You are right. We just need to replace it!" Sparkle said.

"We both are out." Ariel said, pointing at her and Coral.

"Me too." Bella said.

"Same!" Lavender said.

"Fine! I'll drop it." Sparkle sighed.

Chapter Fouteen
Cackle!

Suddenly, they heard shrieking noise.

"Oh no! Cackle, we need to get on our feet! Ariel, you and Coral go to the Council." Sparkle said.

"Yeah, go!" Ariel said.

"Be careful!" Bella said.

They all swam fast, and quickly got on the shore. "Bella, can you tell where we are?" Sparkle asked.

"I think, Shimmer Beach." Bella said, Sparkle nodded.

Suddenly, Cackle, slim and fair, with black and red hair, appeared on a black dragon. "Oh, look who it is, my old friend!" She said mockingly in a shrill voice.

"Drop it, Cackle, I was never your friend, and never will be!" Sparkle said.

"Oh, tough act, hand me the Wand of Power, or it will be the end!"

"No! I don't have the Wand of Power, even if I do, I wouldn't give it to filthy and evil people like you!"

"How dare you!" Cackle shrieked. "Listen you, first you call me by my name, and now you call me filthy? I am downright beautiful! And my forces, are scuba-diving, and attacking your little mermaid friends right now! So, if you surrender, I can tell them to stop."

"Oh no!" Lavender said. "Bella, stay here, I got to…" Her voice trailed away, and she dived.

"Lavender!" Bella said, but Sparkle stopped her from diving.

"Oh, you! Sweetness of yours! Enough to give me a very bad stomachache!" Cackle shrieked. "Anyway, Evils, attack!" Cackle shrieked.

Suddenly, a number of good creatures, on good dragons, Pegasi, Unicorns, and Alicorns came.

"Aunt Petals!" Sparkle shrieked, spotting her on a Pegasi in the crowed. But Aunt Petals motioned her to keep quiet.

"Cackle, we have already send some of our scuba-divers in the water, and mer-creatures are also there, you are powerless, we are many, you are one." The mayor, Ms. Peace said calmly.

"I am not powerless against you, and who says I am alone?" Cackle said and sent black sparks with her wand, and loads of evil creatures on dragons came, trolls also came. There were jinxes, curses and hexes flying everywhere. Sparkle managed to dodge the spells coming her way. When Cackle was busy, Sparkle took the opportunity to check on the sea creatures, she caught the sight of Bella, and motioned her to follow her. When they dived, the water was empty.

"What is this? I... where is everyone. Lavender, Coral and Ariel?" Sparkle asked and panted.

"We have to find them! But Sparkle, you have to go!" Bella said.

"I can't, underwater world needs me!" Sparkle said.

"Underwater world can manage, you manage Cackle!"

"I don't know what to do!" Sparkle said. "This is my first time going into war, and so is yours, but so many innocent lives are at stake! There are even scorpions out there!" Sparkle said.

"I promise no one will die, we are powerful, and so are the sea-creatures, they are all well-hidden."

Sparkle nodded. "We can take this opportunity to sneak into Ghost Land, and free everyone captured by Cackle, we can't bring back the dead, but we can free the innocent from being captive, and tortured!"

"You are right, I know the way, I do my geography homework, unlike you!" Bella said and grinned. Sparkle smiled.

"But around Ghost Land?"

"Yes, I know seven passages, four underwater, three on land."

"Okay, but should we check on Lavender first?"

"I think she will be fine! I mean, she can move plants. Let's go!"

"OK. But which way?" Sparkle asked.

"Follow me. And Sparkle, we might need your invisibility power." Bella said seriously.

"But I can just make *myself* invisible, not you."

"Don't worry, I have a plan!"

Bella quietly swam towards east, as Sparkle followed. Then they came to a silver door. Bella tried opening it, but it didn't.

"The door's not opening!" She cried.

"Try the opening spell!" Sparkle suggested.

"Wait, you try, this might be a trap! Be invisible, unlock the door, and try." Bella said.

"Okay!" Sparkle said as she stepped forward, turned herself invisible with a wave of her hand, took out her wand, which was also now invisible. "*Open Spectorem!*" She said, the door opened, there were two evil-looking mermen standing, both had black hair and dark skin, one was a bit fat, other one thin. Bella hid behind the door.

"Who opened the gate?" The fat one asked the other.

"Don't know!" The other one replied. Sparkle went to Bella, when I touched my wand, it turned invisible, so maybe if I touch you, you can also turn invisible!" Sparkle whispered and held Bella's hand, and she also turned invisible, and they slipped past the guards, they both swam towards the surface, and into an ugly, smokey place. They transformed themselves.

"Eww! So bad, it's so dirty and smokey, even the water!" Sparkle said, holding her nose, and making them visible again.

"Yeah, but let's not focus on that, let's concentrate on finding everyone!" Bella suggested.

"Yeah, you're right!" Sparkle agreed.

They walked towards a huge castle. "I think that's the Cackle Castle, Cackle's castle." Sparkle guessed.

"It sure is, invisible again!" Bella said.

"How will we find our way in that big castle?" Sparkle asked.

"You know, I think we will find it." Bella said confidently.

Sparkle nodded. "So, let's go!" She held Bella's hand and they didn't become invisible. "Why aren't we becoming invisible?"

"I think it only lasts when we are in our mermaid form." Bella said.

"I guess we have to do this the hard way then!" Sparkle said. "We have to sneak past them."

"And how will we do that?" Bella asked.

"We'll see!"

"Okay, this time, I will follow you!"

"Okay!" Sparkle said and begin walking. Then she spotted a guard.

"We can't perform spells here; it will gain attention!" Bella said, who was still hiding behind Sparkle.

Then, a large spider came in front of them. "I am Eclipse, the guardian of Ghost Land, tell me who you are and what are you doing here?" The spider demanded.

"I am Rotty, this is Shadow, we are here to see The Dark Queen Cackle!" Sparkle lied.

"Oh, well! And what about your clothes, and where did you come from?"

"We came in these disgusting clothes because we wanted that no one identify us when we passed that… ugh, Unicorn Kingdom, we are from Russia." Bella said.

"OK. I shall escort you inside. The queen has gone somewhere and will arrive shortly." Eclipse said and took them into the castle. In there were skulls, black roses, and rude messages everywhere.

"This is the main room, our queen will arrive shortly, feel free to explore." Eclipse said. "And take this, the guards will know you are guests." She handed them a red card with black letters, it was written: 'Rotty the guest' and on Bella's: 'Shadow the guest.'

"How did you manage to pull that off, Sparkle?" Bella asked, a soon as Eclipse left the room.

"I just did."

"Okay, now we sneak out!" Bella said.

"We don't need to sneak out, we're guests now." Sparkle said.

"Yes, let's go!" They all searched all the rooms on that floor, but they found nothing.

"Let's *explore* the upper floor!" Bella said with a fake smile.

"Yes." Sparkle said. Whenever any of the guards asked for identification, they both just showed their cards.

"Let's go!" Bella said.

"Yes sure!" Sparkle smiled and darted for the skull staircase ahead.

"Where are you going? Young evils?" A boy a few years older from them with dark-brown hair appeared."

"We were told to explore around. And why do you care anyway?" Bella asked rudely.

"I care! I am the son of the General of the army, and I am provided a secret, important job. Now tell who you are, and why are you here?" He snapped.

Sparkle rolled her eyes. "We are here to meet the Queen of Evils, but she has been delayed. From Russia! We were told to feel free to look around!"

"You can even see our cards!" Bella said and took her card and put it in front of his face.

"Very well then, you may go!"

"Wish you a terrible day!" Bella said.

"Same!"

"I think is has to be here, in a secret room!" Sparkle said.

"Maybe, maybe not."

"Where could it be?"

"Let's search all the rooms here first." Bella suggested.

First, they entered a room, the library and Cackle's study.

"Wow, books everywhere." Bella said and went to reach out to get a book called *how to kidnap sea creatures.* When she pulled it, a door opened from the wall behind.

"Come on! I think they might be in there!" Sparkle said. When they both walked in, she was right! There were merman, sea creatures, and mermaids everywhere in a water tank. The door closed behind them.

"Who are you, and what are you doing here?" One of them asked.

"We are here to rescue you, from Evil Creatures." Sparkle said politely

"Okay, but how can we trust you?" A dragon demanded.

"We have these necklaces. And we didn't steal them, they aren't black!" Bella answered, and they both showed their necklaces.

"Okay, how you open the tanks?"

"We can use the opening spell, but the water will come." Sparkle said.

"Maybe we can…. Open the top of the tanks and help you out from the top?" Bella suggested.

"But that's too high!" A fair, purple-haired mermaid looking like Ariel said.

"There's a ladder here!" Bella said.

"Oh yes, come on Bella, let's climb!" Sparkle said, placing the ladder on one tank.

"Yes, you climb first. I'll take the second one!" Bella said, placing the second ladder. "But how will we free sea dragons, they can't breathe or walk on land!"

"There are only a couple of dragons here! We can… I don't know!"

"We can figure that out later, you can figure that out later now!" Sparkle said crossly as Bella begun climbing.

"Open Spectorem!" Sparkle said, she helped out the mermaid and the baby in the tank. The mermaid transformed. Soon, all the tanks were empty, except the sea dragons,' the girls could

not think of a way to rescue them.

"How to rescue you?" Bella moaned.

"It's okay. Leave us!" One of the oldest dragons said.

"No, how did Cackle bought you here?" Bella asked.

"She put us on a big, moving pool, with wheels, and transferred us, one by one." A smaller dragon answered.

"Okay, we just have to find it." Sparkle said.

"Or maybe, we can use this!" Bella said, and went to get a big cart.

"How will we fill water?" Sparkle asked.

"I can climb to the tank, and take out the water from it, with a mug, and throw the water into the cart."

Bella took out the mug and climbed.

"We can help you!" A merman said.

"Yes, we can also climb, and throw the water, there are enough tanks everywhere, and dragons." Another merman suggested.

"Sure!" Sparkle said, and they did as they said. In twenty minutes, all the carts were filled with water, with dragons in it.

Everyone without a cart took their babies in their hands.

"How will we sneak past them?" A mermaid asked.

"Don't know, wait there a window here!" Bella said and looked down the window. "And there is a staircase on it that leads out!"

"Yes, let's go!" Sparkle said and opened the window.

"It leads to a gate!" Bella said, studying closely. "There are no guards, let's go!"

Sparkle opened the window and went first, almost running. They all followed her.

They all went back to the beach, the sea-creatures dived, while Sparkle stood in front of Cackle, facing her.

"Okay, SPARKLE OCTAVIOUS, WHAT HAVE YOU DONE? She shrieked with rage. "YOU FREED

ALL THE SEA CREATURES?" She asked. Sparkle nodded.

She tried to hit a spell out of her wand, but it didn't react. "You ruined one of my plans, that leaves me powerless for twenty-four hours! You win for now. But you know I will return!" With that, she commanded her forces to retreat. And they left.

Suddenly, Lavender came out of the water. "What happened? You have to fill me in guys!" Lavender said.

"We'll fill you in later!" Bella said, Sparkle went to Aunt Petals.

"Aunt Petals, Uncle Shine, where's Hans?" Sparkle asked.

"I left him I in daycare." Uncle Shine said.

"Sparkle!" Aunt Petals whispered, and bend down. "I think we deserve mom and dad; we love you!" She said softly.

"Yes, sure mom!" Sparkle said in the same tone.

Uncle Shine smiled and hugged Sparkle.

Want to know about Sparkle's next adventure?

Sparkle goes to school next year, but she spots something is odd. The school is new, every fifth year, they go to a special school.

They find a unicorn, pegasi, or an alicorn! And a pet too.

Sparkle notices, that a pair of students; twins, are strange there.

What will happen next?

Find:

SPARKLE'S SPARKLE

And

THE SCHOOL

COMING SOON!

www.ingramcontent.com/pod-product-compliance
Lightning Source LLC
LaVergne TN
LVHW061615070526
838199LV00078B/7295